Contemporary Studies in Literature

Eugene Ehrlich, *Columbia University*
Daniel Murphy, *City University of New York*
  Series Editors

Volumes include:

F. Scott Fitzgerald

a collection of criticism edited by Kenneth E. Eble

McGraw-Hill Book Company

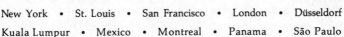

New York • St. Louis • San Francisco • London • Düsseldorf
Kuala Lumpur • Mexico • Montreal • Panama • São Paulo
Sydney • Toronto • Johannesburg • New Delhi • Singapore

2345679MUMU7987654

Library of Congress Cataloging in Publication Data

Eble, Kenneth Eugene, comp.

F. Scott Fitzgerald; a collection of criticism

(Contemporary studies in literature)
CONTENTS: MacKie, E. B. My friend Scott Fitzgerald. —Yates, D. A. The road to "Paradise": Fitzgerald's literary apprenticeship.—Kahn, S. This side of paradise: the pageantry of disillusion. [etc.]

1. Fitzgerald, Francis Scott, 1896–1940.
PS3511.I9Z613   813'.5'2   73-6938
ISBN 0-07-018857-2

Acknowledgments

I wish to thank the authors and the following publications for permission to reprint the articles in this volume: "My Friend, Scott Fitzgerald," by Elizabeth Beckwith MacKie, reprinted from the *Fitzgerald/Hemingway Annual, 1970,* copyright by The National Cash Register Company; "The Road to 'Paradise': Fitzgerald's Literary Apprenticeship," by Donald A. Yates (Spring 1961) and "Fitzgerald and the Simple, Inarticulate Farmer," by J. Albert Robbins (Winter 1961–62), both reprinted from *Modern Fiction Studies; "This Side of Paradise:* The Pageantry of Disillusion," by Sy Kahn reprinted from *The Midwest Quarterly* (January 1966); the section on *The Beautiful and Damned* reprinted from Sergio Perosa, *The Art of F. Scott Fitzgerald,* University of Michigan Press; "Scott Fitzgerald's Fable of East and West," by Robert Ornstein, reprinted from *College English* (December 1956); "The Wasteland of F. Scott Fitzgerald," by John W. Bicknell, reprinted from *The Virginia Quarterly Review* (Autumn 1954); "The Craft of Revision: *The Great Gatsby,*" by Kenneth Eble, reprinted from *American Literature* (November 1964); "Scott Fitzgerald and the 1920's," by Arthur Mizener, reprinted by his permission from *The Minnesota Review* (Winter 1961); *"Tender Is the Night* and the 'Ode to a Nightingale,'" by William E. Doherty, reprinted from *Explorations of Literature* with permission of Louisiana State University Press; "Scott Fitzgerald as Social Novelist: Statement and Technique in 'The Last Tycoon,'" by Michael Millgate, reprinted from *English Studies* (February 1962); and "Fitzgerald at the End," by Midge Decter, reprinted from *Partisan Review* (Spring 1959).

I wish also to thank all those members of my class in F. Scott Fitzgerald, Winter Quarter, 1972, University of Utah. To the graduate students, Lee Ann Beck, Ted Berg, Earl Booth, Bonnie Bobet, Marjorie Coombs, Roger Ekins, Tim Bywater, Jim Force, Jim Hall, Stephen Gould, Susanne Higbee, Sikha Murthy, Clark Passey, Bill Schopf, Marilyn Schroer, Les Standiford, Barbara Terrill, and Kathy Winn, special thanks for their bibliographical work and suggestions about various articles.

Contents

Kenneth E. Eble

Introduction

F. Scott Fitzgerald died in 1940. Since that time, his life has been the subject of three full-length biographies, his life and works have provoked a dozen scholarly books, and his literary remains have been scrutinized closely in hundreds of theses, dissertations, and critical articles. This collection is the fourth of its kind, and there are two separate collections of critical articles dealing with *The Great Gatsby* and *Tender Is the Night.*

Fitzgerald's position in the literary stock market of 1969 is described in the seventh volume of *American Literary Scholarship,* which customarily divides a chapter between Fitzgerald and Hemingway:

> Fitzgerald, whose 1968 showing of thirteen items (plus one for Zelda) was the lowest since 1957, had a respectable thirty-three under his name; but Hemingway soared from forty-seven to eighty-four for 1969, making him the fifth most "popular" American author—after Henry James, Hawthorne, Melville, and Faulkner—in the academic fraternity.[1]

The articles in this collection represent the close, perceptive, informed attention to literary texts characteristic of current literary scholarship. The opening memoir is the only strictly biographical piece in the collection, although few of the critical articles get entirely away from Fitzgerald's life. The critical articles, from Donald A. Yates's summary of Fitzgerald's apprentice

---

[1] J. Albert Robbins, ed., *American Literary Scholarship: An Annual/1969* (Durham, N.C., 1971), p. 122.

1

work to Michael Millgate's discussion of *The Last Tycoon,* provide an introduction to Fitzgerald's writings. Most of these are by comparatively young scholar-critics and are reprinted from literary and scholarly periodicals of the last fifteen years.

The omission of articles by Fitzgerald's near contemporaries —Edmund Wilson, John Peale Bishop, H. L. Mencken, Paul Rosenfeld, and others—is by design. Much of their work is readily available, and the previous collections of critical articles by Alfred Kazin (1951) and Arthur Mizener (1963) have brought much of this material together. For the same reasons, major articles by scholar-critics published shortly after Fitzgerald's death are omitted from this collection. All scholars are in debt to Arthur Mizener's *Far Side of Paradise* (1951; rev. ed., 1965), the first book about Fitzgerald and his work. Similarly, critical articles like those of Malcolm Cowley, Glenway Wescott, William Troy, and Lionel Trilling, established the revival of interest in Fitzgerald's work after his death.

The selection of materials here was guided by a desire to focus upon recent critical articles, to avoid reprinting articles already available in other collections, and to refrain from using portions of books. Even then, the problem remained of selecting from an abundance of materials, for Fitzgerald's writings continue to attract the attention of many gifted younger critics and scholars. For reasons of focus and length, a number of major studies of the past ten years are not included. Matthew Bruccoli's study of the composition of *Tender Is the Night* (1963) is indispensable to an understanding of that book, but nothing short of the study itself can do justice to that complicated subject. Jackson Bryer's various bibliographical studies, both of Fitzgerald's writings and of criticism of his work, are similarly indispensable, but the scope of Bryer's bibliographical work argued against trying to include a summary article. The bibliography at the end of this collection is a selected one, but it includes citations of many recent articles that could well have been included in this collection.

The articles selected represent not only the editor's judgments about the merits of the individual pieces but also his judgments about the relative importance of various works in the Fitzgerald canon and his guesses about what might be of greatest interest to current readers of Fitzgerald's writings. By these standards, there are more articles about Fitzgerald's work in the twenties and more about *The Great Gatsby* than about other periods and works. With two exceptions, all the articles are by American scholars or critics.

This fairly reflects the fact that Fitzgerald has aroused much less interest among foreign critics than has either Hemingway or Faulkner. Nevertheless, Fitzgerald's reputation is international, and one of the selections is reprinted from Sergio Perosa's *L'Arte di F. Scott Fitzgerald* (1961; translated 1965), the only non-English study of Fitzgerald's work to appear as yet. Some of Fitzgerald's novels and stories have been translated into most of the world's major languages, and a body of critical work is beginning to appear in Japan, India, and the European countries in which there is a strong interest in American literature.

The growth of literary scholarship both in America and abroad has strengthened the natural need to reinterpret major authors for each generation of students. For current students in this country, the American twenties are as remote as Victorian England must have been for students of Fitzgerald's time. It is almost impossible, for example, to convince students that descriptions of petting and drinking could have shocked anyone, that *This Side of Paradise* was ever a "sensational" book. Parts of *The Great Gatsby* seem quaint, and much of the Hollywood of *The Last Tycoon* has been auctioned off on studio lots during the past score of years. Even the exotic shadowings and sinister hintings in *Tender Is the Night* may seem dated to some present readers.

Fitzgerald comes to the current generation of students as a writer not yet canonized or fossilized but still placed among the traditional greats. Few students have escaped *The Great Gatsby* or general acquaintance with the legend of Scott and Zelda. And though many students have repudiated American affluence, the American public is still powerfully affected by stories of youthful rise to wealth, power, and fame. In the academic community, serious discussions of Fitzgerald's work have helped shape ideas of American romanticism and the myth of the West for current generations of students. The impact of F. Scott Fitzgerald reaches students of literature both through their own hopes of becoming writers and through the academic constructs by which the generations after Fitzgerald have tried to explain the American experience.

"I was Dick Whittington up from the country gaping at the trained bears."[2] Fitzgerald wrote in 1932, describing his first impressions of New York. The boy from the provinces who made good is the most timeless element in Fitzgerald's life story. Like so many authors who came to prominence in the twenties, he was

---

[2] "My Lost City," in *The Crack-Up,* Edmund Wilson, ed. (New York, 1945), p. 24.

a midwesterner born quite outside a literary or artistic culture. Though he was sent East to a private school and later to Princeton, his immediate family occupied an uneasy social and financial position. His father could trace his ancestry back to southern aristocracy, but it was his mother's Irish family that had amassed solid mercantile wealth.

The provinces, like Catholicism, left their mark upon Fitzgerald. But most of the life and work that preserve his name were compressed into the single decade of the twenties. The publication of *This Side of Paradise,* his marriage to Zelda Sayre, and the achievement of *The Great Gatsby* in 1925 define the first five years. "1000 parties and no work" hang over the last five. From 1924 to 1931, the Fitzgeralds spent more than five years living in Europe. When they returned permanently to the United States in September 1931, Zelda had suffered her first major breakdown, Scott's alcoholism was a confirmed fact, and a novel begun in 1926 and called "Our Type," "The World's Fair," and "The Boy Who Killed His Mother" was still three years away from publication as *Tender Is the Night.*

The end of the story is as grim as the beginning was bright. Zelda's eventual confinement to a sanitarium was only a slightly more marked decline than Fitzgerald's own debilitation in the mid-thirties. Toward the end, there was, for him, something of a comeback. The last years in Hollywood relieved some of his chronic financial problems, brought the columnist Sheilah Graham into his life, and enabled him to do impressive work on his unfinished novel, *The Last Tycoon.* Like many other romantic poets, Fitzgerald died comparatively young, of a heart attack, December 20, 1940. Zelda Fitzgerald died in a fire at Highland Hospital for Nervous Diseases in March, 1948.

The essays in this collection touch upon most of the major themes in Fitzgerald's work and upon his strengths and weaknesses as a writer. Rereading most of the criticism and much of Fitzgerald's work, I am once again struck by the urge to respond to Fitzgerald's writing. Sometimes—often—that response is only an exclamation of delight. Other times it is a need to try to write out a response in one's own words. This is no time, at the end of a brief introduction, to be starting an essay on Fitzgerald. What follows are some jottings occasioned by this encounter with Fitzgerald and his critics.

First, modern criticism (certainly not of Fitzgerald alone) is often too refined. The big things having been said, young critics tend to make too much of small things. Color symbolism, the guest list in *The Great Gatsby*, and the "gat" in "Gatsby" are examples of what one hopes will not dominate criticism of Fitzgerald's work in the future.

Second, there is joy in Fitzgerald's work that should not be passed over in dwelling upon profundities, complexities, and tragic implications. Edmund Wilson described it early as a "quality exceedingly rare among even the young American writers of the day; he is almost the only one among them who has any real light-hearted gaiety."[3] Recognizing that quality and acknowledging its worth may draw attention to the variety to be found in a writer who is commonly charged with having too narrow a range. It also adds to the dimensions of *The Great Gatsby* and *Tender Is the Night*, those novels that do most to maintain Fitzgerald's reputation as a serious writer. For it is not only theme and technique that distinguish these novels, but the flashes of brilliance, comic as well as tragic, that illuminate individual scenes.

Third, Fitzgerald's style, as has been said over and over, is his great strength. Here scholarship has done a great service to Fitzgerald. One's awareness of his style is enhanced by examining the manuscripts through which the finished phrases and paragraphs came into existence. One feels better about one's own strikeovers, and pencilings, and second and third thoughts. One learns. Oddly, few critical articles focus upon Fitzgerald's style, and none of them seemed sufficiently perceptive to warrant inclusion here. The reason for this deficiency is obvious. Fitzgerald, himself, is the best critic of his style; but that criticism does not take the form of analytic examination but rather of notes put down while the writing was in process. "The Note-Books," published in Edmund Wilson's *The Crack-Up*, richly document Fitzgerald's concern for his craft. Anyone daring to write about Fitzgerald's style probably ends up quoting so often that the critic's own intentions get put aside in embarrassment over what little he is contributing.

Fourth, in the presence of so much Fitzgerald scholarship, it is easy to become both solemn and heavy about Fitzgerald, man and work. Perhaps there should be some licensing procedure that would prevent bad writers, pretentious and heavy scholars, from dealing with Fitzgerald. Lacking that, a reader can be grateful

[3] "The Literary Spotlight VI: F. Scott Fitzgerald," *The Bookman*, 55 (March 1922), p. 23.

that, despite some notable exceptions, students as well as professional critics seem attracted to Fitzgerald out of a common respect for his prose style and the storyteller's art. Like Fitzgerald's work, much of Fitzgerald criticism is distinguished by extraordinary felicity of expression.

Finally, Fitzgerald will probably continue to claim the interest of both the general reader and the scholar-critic. The mysteries of his genius, like the mysteries of his style, remain to be pondered. As our own perspectives change, his various works will be seen in different lights. The final test of Fitzgerald, as of all writers, is that others want to read his works and to share the pleasures they receive.

Elizabeth Beckwith MacKie[1]

My Friend Scott Fitzgerald

This is to reverse the usual pattern. I am unable to report (or boast) that during a long friendship with Scott Fitzgerald I ever slept with him. Hardly a month passes but some new, revealing love affair, or indiscretion among the famous, comes out of hiding and into print. And so it is with a proper sense of failure that I cannot add a single flaming episode to tingle the thoughts of that vast hoard who make up Scott's admirers.

It would not have been easy to sleep with Scott, knowing as I did his ideals about the married state, which, when it could have happened, was the case with both of us. It would have destroyed too much. And yet I am not blind to the idea that it might also have brought added beauty to our relationship. There were times when I knew that he needed me, or the physical love and understanding of a woman, and I have let slip the chance to claim even one page for myself from the love life of one of the greats. The truth is that Scott never came right out—wham—and asked me!

It would be unfair to consider Scott Fitzgerald in any light other than a serious one. It would be a misconception of a man whose approach to life was anything but casual. He was dead serious about life, love, art, and friendship, and especially his dedication to his own talent.

We know he often played the clown. His biographers have recorded many such instances, and I saw it happen more times

[1] I am indebted to Henry Dan Piper for much help and advice in the preparation of this reminiscence.

than it is well to remember. But I never saw Scott laugh. I don't remember the sound of his laughter. Even when he was clowning —it was to make others laugh. He was too intent on what he was doing.

The contrast in his pattern of behavior was most noticeable, of course, when he was drinking. He was a man unfitted for the role that fate dealt him (or that he dealt himself). His public image was not the real Scott. When he was drunk he wanted to shock people, and his mind turned inevitably to sex. He would become provocative and suggestive in a way that was a complete reversal of that rather prudish and extremely sensitive, sober Scott. I believe that it was an unconscious effort on his part to equal or excel his wife, the more glittering Zelda. But he was also the victim of a tragic historic accident—the accident of Prohibition, when Americans believed that the only honorable protest against a stupid law was to break it.

I wouldn't have met Scott if it hadn't been for John Peale Bishop. John's family lived six houses and some acres away from our house, on the same street in Charles Town, West Virginia. John, who was twenty-five, was older than most of our group. A childhood illness (some said tuberculosis, but I never really knew) had slowed his progress through school, and so he had only been graduated from Princeton in June 1917. Now he was marking time waiting for the commission in the army that would take him off to officers' training camp.

We knew that John's Princeton friend, Scott Fitzgerald, was arriving for a visit, and my most cherished memento of that visit is a yellowed sheet of paper on which he wrote out for me the sonnet, "When Vanity Kissed Vanity," which he later included in *This Side of Paradise*. On it he wrote "For Fluff Beckwith, the only begetter of this sonnet."

And so the summer, which at the start seemed as routine as all other summers, was soon, in retrospect, to take on added significance by the arrival of a boy, whose name at the time was unimportant, and which I promptly forgot. Scott's visit lasted four weeks, and we were together every day.

Scott and John had entered Princeton together as freshmen in the autumn of 1913. Despite John's being considerably older than most freshmen, and Scott's having been one of the youngest (he was not quite seventeen), they soon became close friends. John, as everyone knows, was the original "Thomas Parke D'Invilliers" in *This Side of Paradise,* and Scott recorded in that novel an amusing account of their first meeting and subsequent friendship.

The contrast between these two personalities makes their friendship all the more interesting and unusual. John lacked Scott's good looks and exuberance. He was perhaps a head taller than Scott, with natural dignity and reserve. His friends were largely selected from the intellectual. My older sister Eloise, was one of his special friends, and he was often at our house. John was a brilliant scholar and prolific poet. In his book of poems *Now With His Love,* he describes a Lely portrait that hung in our home.

He was instinctively attracted to the handsome, impulsive younger boy, who so flatteringly admired his talent. What they shared most of all was a common passion for the life of Art. At Princeton they worked together on the editorial staff of *The Nassau Literary Magazine,* in which they published their undergraduate writings. That eventful summer of 1917 marked the publication of John's first volume of verse, *Green Fruit,* most of which had been previously published in the *Nassau Lit.*

John, like Scott, died too soon. He was fifty-one years old, and as with Scott, his greatest recognition came after death. And so while his literary gift to posterity is limited in quantity, that which he left us is pure beauty. His work becomes more popular each year, and his first full-length novel, *Act of Darkness,* is now being published in paperback.

Scott slipped quietly into Charles Town one afternoon via the dusty old Valley branch of the Baltimore and Ohio railroad, which, except for a limited number of automobiles, was our only escape to the outside world. I had just returned from boarding school in Washington. Our group consisted of boys and girls in their late teens who were home on vacation from school and college. We had all grown up together, and it was our custom to meet almost every day, sometimes in the afternoon for a swim in the nearby Shenandoah River, or for a cross-country ride.

It was July and moonlight—at a party at our house—that I first met Scott. The clematis vine was in full bloom, and the porch railing sagged deeper each year with the weight of the blossoms. The summer air was sweet. I saw him standing in the half shadow watching the dancers. Night had drained the color from his face and hair, and left him pale, but beautiful. He was twenty years old. It was the face of a poet, without sensuality.

We had been dancing to records of "Oh! Johnny" and "Sweethearts," when John came over to me and said, "Fluff, I want you to meet Scott Fitzgerald." It was an appropriate setting and his first words were a parallel of any boy and girl affair that later brought him fame. "I've been watching you," he said, "trying to guess your real name. Is it Eleanor?" "No, Elizabeth," I told him. "Then I was close," he said. "Eleanor—Elizabeth—you see, both names mean pretty much the same kind of girl."

It wasn't until I had known him for several days, and watched him with other people, that I realized that other girls all got the same carefully rehearsed treatment. But this discovery, instead of disillusioning me, merely increased my interest in him. Scott was that rare individual that went out of his way to make each girl feel very special. In a way it was nothing but a "line"—except that most boys' lines are quickly recognizable for what they are. What made Scott's different was the mixture of art and sincerity that went into every performance. He really wanted each girl to be pleased and flattered, and to respond to him, and she usually did.

The next thing I knew we were dancing together. The best description of his dancing I can think of is "lively." He had a sense of rhythm and was easy to follow, but he never attempted any trick steps. He liked to talk while he danced, and he enjoyed having a captive audience. But I liked only to feel the lovely close union of body and music, and I found it difficult to concentrate on what he was saying. But suddenly I was listening. I heard him say, "Townsend said he hoped I would meet you."

Townsend Martin was a classmate of John's who had visited him in June. He was a cosmopolite of great charm and elegance, and I was dazzled from the beginning. It was an affair that started and ended within safe range of the bridge table, but he soon cast cold water on my hopes by announcing that he was descended from "a long line of bachelors." This was a deflating experience for a girl who traditionally thought of "belledom" as the only way of life. A new boy, a new interest, was needed to help restore a drooping ego. Afterwards, in my diary for that night of July 2, I wrote: "I met John's guest. He is good looking. He asked me for a date. We are going on a picnic tomorrow."

I remember patting my cheeks with a piece of wet pink crepe paper that next afternoon. My parents disapproved of cheek rouge as "too fast," and instead of black cotton swimming stockings, I wore my best black silk ones. Chaperones were still *de rigeur,* and our social life was organized around the rule that there was safety in numbers. We were still passionately innocent. If the picnic lasted into the tempting hours of darkness, a chaperone appeared at dusk and joined the group until we were safely back at home.

Scott showed up in his bathing suit, and I surveyed him discreetly but approvingly. He wasn't terribly tall, but was strong and well-knit. And he was carrying a book. But what struck me most was his hat. I had never seen a boy go swimming with a hat. He explained that he burned so badly that he had to keep his skin covered up from the sun. And it was true. If he wasn't careful he turned a painful scarlet. He was a good swimmer, but out of the water we sat in the shade most of time because of his tender skin.

For those of us who lived near the Shenandoah River and loved it, it wound through our lives as between its own banks. Scott soon learned to share our affection for the river, and its many moods. We knew it by heart: one minute flowing blue and lazy, the next a muddy torrent churned by a sudden mountain thunderstorm. We knew the danger spots, and the holes for diving, and the islands where the snakes were thickest. The hidden inlets—just wide enough for a canoe. The gentle rapids where it was so shallow we could lie on our stomachs, and be tossed from rock to rock. And the soft night sounds, broken by song, and echoes on the water.

When the sun dropped behind the Blue Ridge Mountains, Scott and I would drift downstream in a canoe. But the canoes were small, and too crowded for a chaperone—she sat on the bank. Most of the time I listened while he talked and talked. He loved to say things to you that would shock you, just to get your reaction and explain it so accurately that you felt completely exposed. His conversation was mainly about girls. He was always trying to see how far he could go in arousing your feelings, but it was always with words.

"Fluff, have you ever had any 'purple passages' in your life?" he asked me. I wasn't sure what it meant, but it sounded exciting. I always expected the questions to develop a more physical tone. The tingling excitement of a mood, slowly developed, yet surely building toward an exquisite moment. But this was his first exposure to southern girls, who in turn had been exposed to less timid southern boys. The southern boys I knew, despite their verbal lethargy, at least understood what it was all about, and were more aggressive and emotionally satisfying. In 1917, I'm afraid, Scott just wasn't a very lively male animal.

No photograph I have ever seen of him has captured successfully the remarkable sensitivity of his expression. It was like quicksilver. His eyes, contrary to what others have said, were neither green nor blue, but gray-blue. His hair in the sunlight was shining gold. His mouth was his most revealing feature—stern, with thin lips. The upper lip had a slight curve to it, but the lower lip was a stern, straight line. All his Midwestern puritanism was there. He had never lived in that magnetic world of the senses, whose inhabitants communicate by a wordless language of intuitive feelings.

In general, however, Scott's visit to Charles Town was a small social triumph. He was in demand for all the parties, and seemed to enjoy our unsophisticated small-town amusements—and during that month I never saw him take a drink.

Much activity centered around horses. I had been proudly raised with the knowledge that one of my forebears, Sir Marmaduke Beckwith, had been responsible for introducing the first English race-horses into Virginia. Scott had no such feelings about horses or horseback riding—a fact that the horse under him immediately grasped. Scott was a terrible horseman, but determined to ride at all costs. Once he was given an old nag who habitually bolted for home whenever he passed a certain familiar corner. Scott took a bad spill, but got up dusty and determined, and insisted on climbing back on. We all cheered and admired his courage, but it was clear he would never make a good horseman.

One evening just before he left Charles Town, he told me, "Fluff, I've written a poem for you," and he recited "When Vanity Kissed Vanity."

I felt chilly when he came to the line "and with her lovers she was dead." "Do you mean you think I'm going to die?" "No," he replied, "I mean you're dead to me because your other lovers have taken you from me." Later, when Edmund Wilson edited the posthumous volume of pieces called *The Crack-Up,* he published a letter Fitzgerald had written to him. It included the same sonnet, only this time with the title "To Cecilia." It was a great disappointment at first. Still, the girl was his cousin, and fourteen years older, and besides Scott had given it two months earlier to me.

August came too soon, and Scott returned to his home in St. Paul, Minnesota. And several weeks later, while I was on a trip to New York, friends introduced me to the young man who would soon afterwards marry me and share my life for the next forty-two years. Paul and I first met in Peacock Alley of the old Waldorf-Astoria, on 34th Street, a romantic encounter that Scott would surely have appreciated.

Looking back over the vista of fifty years to that eventful summer when I first met Scott. I know that he could never have been happy with small-town life. He was in search of wider hori-

For [illegible] Beckwith, the only begotten of his sonnet — Scott Fitzgerald

When Vanity kissed Vanity
— a hundred happy Junes ago
He drank her beauty breathlessly
and
(that all time would always know)
He rhymed her eyes with Life and Death
"Thru time I'll save my love," he said
.... but Beauty vanished with his
breath
And, with her lovers, she was dead

— Ever his wit & not her eyes
Ever his heart & not her hair
"Who'd learn a trick in rhyme, be wise
and pause before his sonnet there"
So all my words, however true
might rhyme you thru a thousand Junes
and no one ever knew That you
were Beauty for an afternoon.

Collection of the late Elizabeth Beckwith MacKie.

zons. He failed to discover the real core of small-town life — or its rewards. Small towns are people — there is little else. A place where one comes close to the pulse of human emotion. We learned early about life and living from some of the most beloved members of the colored race — exciting, intimate things, because we were not ashamed to ask. Their wisdom was earthy and uncluttered, and with the sharp intuition of their race. "That ain't no way to ketch yessef a man, you got to pleasure him, honey, you got to pleasure a man." "The apple falls close to the tree." "The sweetest smell of all ain't no smell at all." I could go on and on. In the end we were gentler and wiser.

We were all excited when *This Side of Paradise* was published in the spring of 1920. John Bishop told me that Scott had said I was his model for Eleanor in the section called "Young Irony." When I read it I remembered our first meeting and Scott's having told me that Eleanor and Elizabeth were names that suggested to him the same kind of girl. I saw a vague resemblance to myself in his description of Eleanor's "green eyes and nondescript hair," and there were Amory's and Eleanor's horseback rides through mountain paths together, and the rural setting which was so obviously inspired by the country around Charles Town. And there was, of course, my poem. But the Eleanor he described only reminded me of how little he really knew me. His Eleanor loved to sit on a haystack in the rain reciting poetry. Forgive me, Scott: if that is the way you wanted it, then you missed the whole idea of what can happen atop a haystack.

It wasn't until fourteen years later, in the early spring of 1932, that I saw him again. By 1932 it seemed as though Zelda had almost recovered from her 1930 collapse. Then, that winter after her father died, she had a second mental breakdown, and Scott brought her from Alabama to Johns Hopkins Hospital in Baltimore for treatment. By spring she was well enough to be released from the hospital, but her physician wanted her to remain nearby for observation and therapy.

Scott was staying temporarily in a Baltimore hotel, looking for a house to rent for Zelda and himself and eleven-year-old Scottie. Scott liked the idea of settling in Baltimore, after having spent the last ten years on and off in Europe. He no longer wanted to go back to St. Paul. On his father's side, the Fitzgeralds had lived in eastern Maryland for generations, and his father, who had recently died, was buried in the family plot at nearby Rockville. Besides, a number of his old Princeton friends were Baltimoreans.

One of his classmates, Bryan Dancy, lived next door to us. Bryan and his wife Ida Lee knew that I had once known Scott. So when they heard he was in Baltimore, they invited my husband and me to have dinner with him. A lot had happened since I had last seen Scott. He was now a celebrity, and he was at the height of his popular career. *The Great Gatsby* had not only been a highly praised novel, but also a Broadway play and a Hollywood motion picture. Besides, Scott was one of the highest-paid magazine writers of the day; *The Saturday Evening Post* featured his stories regularly. We had learned vaguely of Zelda and her illness. But most of the details were veiled in mystery, and hardly anyone in Baltimore knew her.

When Paul and I arrived at the Dancys' for dinner, Scott was standing in the living room. I paused for a moment, puzzled by what I saw. There were two Scotts: the old Scott of memory—the other, very drunk. He had run into a second-string Hollywood movie actress staying at his hotel (she was well-known then, but has since died and long been forgotten), and impetuously decided to bring her. They had tarried in the bar too long. She had said she was lonely and knew no one in Baltimore, and Scott felt sorry for her, and told her to come along. It was a chaotic evening. Scott had obviously decided to make it so, and to confirm his reputation as an unconventional guest. The more vulnerable we appeared, the sharper the attack, with realistic allusions to feminine curves and their function. It was a rejection of the Scott I had known.

As we got up from dinner he started for the front door. He struck a dramatic pose and said: "I am going home—to satisfy a need—the need for sex." He disappeared through the door, followed by the actress.

I was not entirely unprepared for this behavior. I had heard occasionally over the years from John Bishop, who had briefed me on many of the Fitzgeralds' more spectacular exploits in Europe. Compared to the fireworks that flared much of the time around Scott and Zelda, John's life was stable. In 1930 he had won Scribners' prize for his story, "Many Thousands Gone." He and his wife Margaret lived quietly as expatriates in a chateau in France, and were the parents of three sons.

All over America drinking was becoming more and more a social habit. But the rest of us had routine responsibilities, our daily jobs to attend to, and our lives were well-organized. Scott was much more of a free agent. There had been nothing of this routine to restrain him, and by the time he came to Baltimore, he had become incapable of controlling his drinking. It magnified the minor flaws in his personality, and erased the charm and good manners.

When Arthur Mizener came to Baltimore in search of Fitzgerald material for his biography of Scott, I hid. I could not at that time discuss my friendship with Scott without, I feared, hurting him. I preferred the privacy of non-recognition. How times have changed. But in spite of that unfortunate meeting, Scott and I eventually got back to a firmer relationship. No matter how badly he behaved, Scott was always sincerely sorry afterwards and would atone by a charming apology. His manners were still beautiful. Physically, he had changed very little during the last fourteen years. He was such a delightful, sensitive person, that my husband Paul, who was rather correct and strait-laced, recovered from his first impression and took a liking to him.

Apart from the drinking, I recognized the same old Scott, but a more retiring Scott than I had known before. He discouraged social invitations, much to the disappointment of the many Baltimore hostesses who had hoped to enliven their parties with such a well-known personage. Zelda, of course, was too ill most of the time to go out in public, but Scott used her illness as an excuse to dodge social entanglements. And deep, deep down he never forgot to love her.

I had not met Zelda before, and saw her only a few times during her stay in Baltimore. I knew that she had once been very beautiful. John Bishop had written me after her wedding that "she looked like an angel." Now her shoulders drooped and her skin was pallid, but there was about her still a wistful, feminine charm. One afternoon she dropped by to call, and told me she had been shopping all day for a dress with a hood in back. I remember wondering at the time if this was her way of disguising her slouching posture. Another time she invited Ida Lee Dancy and me to lunch at their home, "La Paix." She kept us waiting for an hour. And when she finally showed up, rather damp-looking, she told us that she had been in the bathtub—that part of her therapy consisted of taking a long sitz-bath to relax her nerves, with a big thermometer to make sure the water stayed the right temperature. She talked freely about her illness.

Scott often dropped by our house for a casual visit. The visits I remembered with the most pleasure were those when, as he expressed it, he was "on the wagon." The length of these dry spells varied, but they sometimes lasted a month or more. It was during these visits that he often discussed the literary talents of the writers he had known, and he had interesting comments on many of the movie greats of that day. With his usual generosity toward other authors, he told me that Thomas Wolfe was the most gifted writer of his generation. If we were out, he would leave an amusing note —invariably addressed jointly to my husband and me. He liked to drop in unannounced. But he almost always refused invitations to formal parties—especially when there might be lots of people whom he didn't know. He lacked the interest to make new acquaintances, and preferred old friends. At one of our cocktail parties to which he came, he was immediately surrounded by a circle of admiring, gushing women. When he finally escaped, he told me, "God, I'm sick of all those teeth grinning at me."

So although we continued to invite him, we soon grew accustomed to his polite letters of apology. After he failed to show up, we would sometimes find a note tucked in the front screen door, like the following, dated July 1933:

> Don't expect me
>   I've gone fancy
> I'm all set
>   With Bryan Dancy
> Scotty's Windbag
>   Mitchell's Berries
> Back at midnight
> Out with Fairies

My last recollection of Scott is in June, 1936. His current plans were to visit Zelda, who was now convalescing in a private sanitarium in North Carolina, and then go out to Hollywood to write for the motion pictures. As things turned out, he was injured while diving in a pool at a hotel in Asheville, and as a result of his having to be hospitalized, his departure for Hollywood was delayed until the following summer of 1937. At the time of our next-to-last meeting, however, he was planning to leave not only Baltimore but the east coast for good. Scott had come to our house to tell us his plans, and to say that he was leaving as soon as he could get rid of some furniture stored in the Monumental Warehouse in Baltimore.

Paul and I were then spending our summers in the country, and needed furniture, and so Paul bought from Scott a pair of twin beds and a painted chest of drawers. The next day I went to the warehouse. I remember how depressed I was by most of the things —they all looked as though no one had cared very much for them

for a long time. I bought one more piece, a bureau, and so I went
to the apartment in the Cambridge Arms, to which he and Scottie
had moved temporarily, to give him a check.

It was lunch time, but Scott was still in pajamas and bathrobe.
He was entertaining Louis Azrael, a well-known local newspaper
columnist. He also had a severe pain in his shoulder, which he had
relieved by the home remedy of strapping an electric heating pad
to his back, and he was sitting on the floor plugged into the electric
current. Always restless, and always the perfect host, he would
get up from the floor and wander about with plug and cord clatter-
ing behind him. But there was also a wonderful dignity flowing
from him that repulsed any sympathy of mine and that gave him
a kind of tragic grandeur.

This was my farewell to Scott. I would never again see his
handsome face, or hear him say, as he once did, when he was leaving our house and the screen door was safely between us, "Fluff,
I've never had you, but I believe we always get the things we most
want."

His popularity was beginning to go into temporary decline.
Shortly after his death I read an obituary by Margaret Marshall in
The Nation, February, 1941. She wrote of Scott: "A man of talent
who did not fulfill his early promise—his was a fair-weather talent
which was not adequate to the stormy age into which it happened,
ironically, to emerge."

Today Scott Fitzgerald is required reading in many schools
and colleges, and my grandchildren come with school assignments,
wanting to learn more about him. I show them my original copy
of the sonnet, "When Vanity Kissed Vanity"—once so lightly received, and now so dearly treasured—when there is no longer
cause for vanity. And one of them asked, "Grandmother, did you
really kiss Scott Fitzgerald?"

Heavens! No one ever *thought* of such things in those days.
Well—hardly ever.

Donald A. Yates

The Road to "Paradise": Fitzgerald's Literary Apprenticeship

If there are no such persons as "born writers," F. Scott Fitzgerald was the next best thing. He was a "born observer." To this quality he brought a youthful self-confidence and an unwavering conviction that he could produce out of his own head stories as entertaining as any he had read. He preserved this egotism, almost intact, up to the time when he published *This Side of Paradise.* Between 1909, the date of his first published work, and 1920, the date of *Paradise,* he was not consciously preparing himself for a career as a novelist; but the surprisingly large amount of writing he did during the years leading up to his first popular success nonetheless contributed toward that end. The individual pieces which he composed during his early years—stories, plays, poetry, satire, and even song lyrics—run close to one hundred in number. It is evident, therefore, that the sudden success of his first novel was only to a small degree ascribable to chance. Fitzgerald had actually had an extensive apprenticeship.

Why did the young boy from St. Paul write? In the beginning it was to please himself. Later, he wrote to please others with the inventions of his imagination. At Princeton, for a while, writing for publication was, as he saw it, the thing to do. Finally, in his last fifteen months at school, following a severe set-back to his youthful ambitions, and as a result of the influence of several "literary" classmates, he found in writing not only something to believe in, but something eminently worth *living for.* The author's pre-1920 writings tell this story.

Reprinted from Modern Fiction Studies, *VII (Spring 1961), 19–31, by permission,* © *1961, by Purdue Research Foundation, Lafayette, Indiana.*

I

Fitzgerald's first published work, "The Mystery of the Raymond Mortgage," appeared in the September 1909 issue of the *Now and Then*. This was the school publication of the St. Paul Academy, a local country day school which he was then attending. He had written other things before—a play at the age of seven and a story of knighthood at the age of ten, among other pieces—but these are lost now. However, we have no reason to suppose that they were unlike "The Raymond Mortgage" with respect to its marked degree of imitation of other models. The style of Conan Doyle and touches of LeBlanc pervade this story about a double murder and the theft of a "valuable mortgage." There is the bumbling chief of police and the bright newspaperman who solves the case. There is a butler (who is killed) and clues (footprints and spent bullets) and complications too elaborate for the story to support. There are implausibilities: a dead woman is left at the scene of the crime for four days while the investigation proceeds. (At this early stage, the young writer found it necessary to evoke a new day for each new development.) Yet, despite its extravagant weaknesses and flaws, the story has undeniable color and a good sense of movement. Since it is the most complex of Fitzgerald's early stories, perhaps more than anything else it reveals the young writer's serious concern over *plot*. This is an interesting point; for if Fitzgerald's subsequent *Post* stories suffer from one consistent fault, this fault is overplotting.

Between 1910 and 1911, Fitzgerald wrote three more stories for the *Now and Then*. One was a simple football anecdote entitled "Reade, Substitute Right Half," in which a "light haired stripling" strongly resembling the would-be football hero, Fitzgerald, saves the day with a brilliant run. The other two stories, "A Debt of Honor" and "The Room with the Green Blinds," are Civil War tales which turn on rather dramatic surprise endings.

Most of these reflect the *imitative* side of the young writer. They suggest to us the type of books he was reading and the sort of stories that he was hearing from his father, who was fond of recounting tales of the Civil War. These were adventures fashioned by the same Scott who invented games for the neighborhood children to play. Characteristically, these pieces had little to do with life as he was observing it. At the same time, however, he was keeping a personal record of his observations—prose jottings which came closer than any of these fictions to expressing his intimate feelings. This record, which Fitzgerald called his "Thoughtbook," foreshadows some of his best pages.

The "Thoughtbook," kept between 1910 and 1911, was a sort of adolescent's diary, in which were recorded the random and baffling shiftings of favor which describe the eternal drama churned up between youthful members of the opposing sexes. Fitzgerald was a very shrewd observer of these trends. Because popularity meant so much to him, and possibly because he was fascinated by its fickle nature, he proved to be a considerably gifted teen-aged sociologist in these matters. The "Thoughtbook," which he divided into chapters, contains lists of favorite boys and girls. (At one point, he enters the proviso: "This list changes continually. Only authentic at date of chapter.") It also contains descriptions of specific incidents involving his young friends. A good illustration of Fitzgerald's natural style and dramatic insight is given in Chapter IX, dated August, 1910.

> Kitty Williams is much plainer to my memory. I met her first at dancing school and as Mr. Van Arnum (our dancing teacher) chose me to lead the march I asked her to be my pardner. The next day she told Marie Louty and Marie repeated it to Dorothy Knox who in turn passed it on to Earl that I was third in her affections. I don't remember who was first but I know that Earl was second and as I was already quite overcome by her charms I then and there resolved that I would gain first place. As in the case of Nancy there was one day which was preeminent in my memory. I went in Honey Childenton's yard one morning where the kids usually congregated and beheld Kitty. We talked and talked and finally she asked me if I was going to Robin's party and it was there that my eventful day was. We played postoffice, pillow, clappin and clapp out and other foolish but interesting games. It was impossible to count the number of times I kissed Kitty that afternoon. At any rate when we went home I had secured the coveted 1st place. I held this until dancing school stopped in the spring and then relinquished it to Johnny Gowns a rival. On valentines day that year Kitty received no less than eighty four valentines. She sent me one which I have now as [and] also one which Nancy gave me. Along in a box with them is the lock of hair—but wait I'll come to that. That Christmas I bought a five pound box of candy and took it around to her house. What was my surprise when Kitty opened the door. I nearly fell down with embarrassment but I finally stammered "Give this to Kitty," and ran home.

This excerpt from the "Thoughtbook" represents what Fitzgerald, even at an early age, could do well: observe people and their interrelationships, project himself into their midst, and capture the essence of his experiences in objective and dramatic terms. His obsession with popularity and his attention to the relative ranking of his friends, to be sure, is a facet of the personality of the young egotist. But it is also true that this preoccupation with the standards and procedures of society carries through to the best of his novels and stories written in the two decades that lay ahead of him.

If the passage dedicated to Kitty Williams seems laced with ambition and self-assurance, it should readily be accepted as characteristic of the boy. It appears that Fitzgerald was a kind of neighborhood Belasco, an irrepressible entertainer. He was always dreaming up things for others to do. In view of this, it seems apparent that his early writings were not produced out of a desire for publication and fame. It is likely that what he wrote during this period was strictly for his own pleasure—be it the pleasure of accomplishment or that pleasure he received indirectly from observing that his fictions were amusing his young friends and, in some cases, grownups as well.

One of the adults who were most dazzled by the young Fitzgerald was Miss Elizabeth Magoffin of St. Paul, under whose patronage he wrote, in August of 1911, a short play entitled *The Girl from the Lazy J.*[1] This was the first in a series of four plays that Fitzgerald wrote for production by the Elizabethan Dramatic Club, which was headed by Miss Magoffin.

The Girl from the Lazy J is a western. It has a cast of five characters, a number of rather awkward soliloquies, and a minimum of motivated plot action. The plot centers on the drama inherent in concealed identities (a theme Fitzgerald was to exploit in subsequent plays). The manuscript carries Miss Magoffin's superficial corrections; but it is apparent that she was but lightly critical with her "young genius."

That fall, the boy's parents, with the financial help of an aunt, sent him to the Newman School at Hackensack, New Jersey. He had not proved himself either a popular fellow (he was considered too "fresh") or a diligent student at the Academy, and his enrollment at Newman was intended to to be a means to get him straightened out and studying. But at Newman, too, his brightness and

[1] This play and those written for production in the summers of 1913 and 1914 have been believed lost. But copies of *The Girl from the Lazy J, Coward,* and *Assorted Spirits*—copied out in Miss Magoffin's hand—are now located among the Fitzgerald papers at the Firestone Library in Princeton.

freshness soon made him a marked man among his classmates. Nor did he turn over a new leaf academically. He continued to write secretly and sought his chief stimulation outside the classroom, in the New York theaters where he saw and was greatly impressed by his first Broadway shows. The only record that remains of the writing he did during his first year at Newman is the thirty-six line poem entitled "Football," which was published in the *Newman News*.[2]

The shows he attended on Broadway ultimately had their effect. In the spring of 1912, on his way back home to St. Paul on the train, Fitzgerald wrote a new play which he entitled *The Captured Shadow*.

II

The Captured Shadow was presented by the Elizabethan Dramatic Club in August of 1912. To judge from a reading of the manuscript as we have it in young Fitzgerald's own hand, it must indeed have been a successful play. It is undoubtedly the best piece of dramatic writing that he had done up to this time. The play flows along very well; there is a particularly good opening and development in the first act; there are smooth entrances and exits; and there is a considerable amount of movement and action. The humor of the opening scene (arising from the extraction of juicy bits of information from an eavesdropping domestic by the "indignant" mistress who had surprised the servant in the act) must have amused the audience. The scene obviously amused Fitzgerald. Moreover, it suggests that he had learned something important about dramatic technique: that the audience takes delight in being given a conversation from which, through insights lent by the author, it can extract more meaning than is apparent on the surface.

The story is essentially an imitation of the type of melodrama that had so impressed the young author in the plays he saw in New York. The hero might have sprung full-blown straight out of *Alias Jimmy Valentine*. The sense of the gallant roguery of Arsène Lupin

---

[2] Fitgerald's football "obsession," which makes itself evident early in his life, often found expression in what he wrote. His dream of football glory was a persistent illusion, one which he cherished for another twenty-five years. For an examination of this facet of the author's personality, see the present writer's "Fitzgerald and Football," *Michigan Alumnus Quarterly Review*, Fall, 1957.

(one of Fitzgerald's early heroes) is manifest throughout the play. However, together with the influences of his models the young playwright mixed in some of his own favored brand of entertainment. There is interpolated a whole series of timeless childhood jokes and vaudeville gags which "keeps the show loose," so to speak. Some examples: a character stammers, "But-but-but-" and is cut off with the ill-conceived quip, "You talk like a goat!" (which probably drew a laugh anyway); someone comments that a certain loud suit looks cheap and the wearer promptly replies, "Why it's all covered over with checks!"

The mystery play is not fair in the placing and follow-up of clues, but it would seem that no one took note of the fact. There is a pleasant little romance woven into the drama which is resolved with a good final line (a Fitzgerald trademark) when the "Captured Shadow," revealed as a celebrated society figure in disguise, admits that he has succumbed to the heroine's charms and now is indeed a truly "captured" Shadow.[3]

Fitzgerald returned to Newman that fall with an apparent dedication to try to get the things he wrote into print. Now on the editorial staff of the *Newman News,* he made a total of five contributions to the magazine during 1912–1913, which was his last year at the school. Two of these pieces, "Election Night" and "School Dance," are merely brief observations which serve only to indicate Fitzgerald's interest in the social functions of the school. The remaining three items are short stories. Of these, "Pain and the Scientist" is a simple anecdote with a meager amount of trimming. It deals with a man who has become angered at the attitude of his Christian Scientist neighbor who tries to convince him that there is no such thing as pain. The story ends with the neighbor's "comeuppance": after lecturing the protagonist on his childish attitude toward pain, he has an accident and is obliged to beg his "pupil" to release him from his discomfort. It is a slight little tale.

The two other stories represent an important step forward both in the writer's development and in his search for the "right" material. "A Luckless Santa Claus" deals with a wealthy young man who takes up his fiancée's bet that he cannot *give away* twenty-five dollars on Christmas Eve. To his dismay, he finds he cannot do it. "On the Trail of the Duke" is also a "plotted" story

---

[3] A fairly close account of the 1912 production of this play is given in Fitzgerald's story "The Captured Shadow," which appeared in the December 29, 1928 *Post.* The story is included in *Taps at Reveille* and in Malcolm Cowley's selection of Fitzgerald's stories (*The Stories of F. Scott Fitzgerald:* Scribners, 1951).

which concerns a young beau who is sent by his girl friend to
search for a missing duke who has wandered away from her house.
The fellow has heard that a French duke had been visiting and assumed that this was whom he was to look for. He returns many
hours later empty-handed, only to find that the "Duke" was his
girl's missing poodle, which has since returned. These two stories,
executed in similar style, are remarkably well carried off. They
offer proof that Fitzgerald was learning some things about the art
of writing prose.

But perhaps more significant than the lively descriptions, the
charming and convincing dialogue, the increasing sensitivity towards his characters—all of which are evident here—is the fact
that Fitzgerald had discovered material for which he had a definite feeling: he had chosen to deal with comfortably wealthy
young people of his own time. He was, as we know, exceptionally
well equipped to explore in this area of society. Seven years later
he would publish a first novel that is peopled with young men and
women of similar social and economic status.

In these *Newman News* stories published during the year pre-
ceding his arrival at Princeton we already glimpse clear flashes of
the future moralistic writer of fables about the young and the rich.
Consider, from "A Luckless Santa Claus," the following:

> In the parlor of a house situated on a dimly lighted residential street
> somewhere east of Broadway, sat the lady who . . . started the
> whole business. She was holding a conversation half frivolous, half
> sentimental, with a faultlessly dressed young man who sat with her on
> the sofa. All this was quite right and proper, however, for they were
> engaged to be married in June.

And this paragraph from "On the Trail of the Duke":

> In his house on upper Fifth Avenue, young Dodson Garland lay on a
> divan in the billiard room and consumed oceans of mint juleps, as he
> grumbled at the polo that had kept him in town, the cigarettes, the
> butler, and occasionally breaking the Second Commandment. The
> butler ran back and forth with large consignments of juleps and soda
> and finally, on one of his dramatic entrances, Garland turned towards
> him and for the first time that evening perceived that the butler was a
> human being, not a living bottle-tray.

The importance of Fitzgerald's discovery of the charms of
writing about his own time and about his own "generation" is dem-

onstrated by the fact that henceforth, until the publication of *This Side of Paradise,* he wrote only two stories that did not have contemporary backgrounds. And after *Paradise* his fame as a short-story writer was based on the portraits of his own "creations"— the flapper and her beaux.

In St. Paul, in the late summer of 1913, just a month before he appeared on the Princeton campus, his third play written for the Elizabethan Dramatic Club was presented. The title was *Coward,* and Fitzgerald returned to the Civil War period for his scene. It is the most ambitious of his juvenile plays. The cast contains seventeen characters who are deployed over two acts (with an interim time lapse of three years) with an undeniable dramatic sense. Once again the opening is effective, and once more the exits and entrances are smoothly managed. The plot is developed around the occupation of a Virginia home by Yankee soldiers. (The author's bias favors the South.) A Southerner who in the first act demonstrates himself a coward is redeemed by curtaindrop in the second. The resolution of a long-pending romance provides the curtain line, as it did in *The Captured Shadow.* Playing on the title of the drama, Fitzgerald has the hero Holworthy confess to having been —three years before—a "coward" in romance as well as in battle.

For all of its implausibilities and youthful excesses, the play appears to have been a success. A subsequent "command" performance was given on September 12 at the nearby White Bear Yacht Club at Dellwood, Minnesota; and for the second time in five days the young Fitzgerald received the enthusiastic approval of his audience and of the local press. This glory must have seemed sufficient to last for a while, for there is no record of Fitzgerald's having written anything for publication or performance during the next year—until the presentation in September of 1914 of his last play for the Elizabethan Dramatic Club. While at Newman, he had learned about a theatrical group at Princeton called the Triangle Club which staged original operettas. We have his own words to the effect that he chose Princeton primarily in order to play on the Tiger football team and, secondly, in order to be able to write for Triangle. He failed on his first day out to make the Princeton freshman football team, and therefore likely poured all his energies into work on the 1914–1915 Triangle show. To this single-minded dedication we must attribute the silence from September of 1913 to September of the following year.

III

Fitzgerald's attendance at Princeton between fall of 1913 and November of 1917 is properly divided into two distinct periods. He attended steadily from September of 1913 through November of 1915 when he left school owing to a combination of health and academic problems. He returned in September of 1916 as a junior and as a member of the Class of '18. He had fallen a year behind his original class. This setback had a lasting effect on him. What he wrote before and after this reversal should properly be considered as belonging to two distinct phases of his development as a writer.

During his first year at Princeton Fitzgerald worked a great deal on the book and lyrics for the Triangle show, *Fie! Fie!, Fi-Fi!* At the same time he was beginning to associate with several literarily inclined young men from whom he felt he could learn many things about this exciting thing called the English language. He now spent time with young poets and dedicated intellectuals such as John Peale Bishop and Edmund Wilson. His classes were of less importance to him than his new friends; they and the Triangle lyrics kept him away from many of his lectures. Consequently, his freshman year was not an unqualified academic success, and he was obliged to report to Princeton early in the fall of 1914 to make up several class deficiencies. He still found time, however, to write and polish up his fourth and final drama for the Elizabethan Dramatic Club—a two-act farce entitled *Assorted Spirits.* It appears in the reading to be the least successful of the St. Paul plays. As before, he had found himself a common enough plot (a house is made to seem haunted in order to reduce its sale price) and he once again inserted a simple little romance; but the play seems to lack the exuberant spirit of the earlier pieces. Perhaps he had temporarily lost interest in the dramatic form, perhaps he turned out the play merely because it was expected of him. Whatever the reason, we cannot doubt that his imagination was racing ahead to the fall in anticipation of the work remaining to be completed on the Triangle show.

In September he passed off his conditions and was accepted as a sophomore, although he was not allowed to take part officially in Triangle activities. His ultimate contribution to *Fie! Fie!, Fi-Fi!* consisted of seventeen song lyrics. Taken as a group, they strike one as being competently executed; but one sees little of Fitzgerald in them and much of W. S. Gilbert. Now barred from full participation in the Triangle presentation, he decided to go home for the holidays while the show went on tour. In St. Paul, as it happened, he had a more significant experience than he likely could ever have had traveling with the Triangle group. Near the end of the vacation he met and fell desperately in love with a girl from Westover by the name of Ginevra King. She would serve as the model for the emancipated, desirable but elusive young heroine in much that Fitzgerald wrote up until the time of the publication of *This Side of Paradise.* She gave substance to the vague, faceless "society girl" that he had already begun to describe.

By the following spring Fitzgerald had adjusted himself well enough to the Princeton environment to be able to get down to some serious writing. In the April 1915 issue of the *Nassau Lit,* the school literary magazine, he published a story written in dramatic form called "Shadow Laurels." It showed that he had absorbed quite a bit from his friends, if not from his teachers, concerning the business of writing. The scene of the story is a wine shop in Paris. A trio of neighborhood *habitués* are approached by a stranger who is inquiring into the facts surrounding the death of his father who, many years before, had died in that part of Paris. The young man had always believed that his father had been a failure and that his death must have occurred under sordid circumstances. The three local customers immediately recall the father and assure the son that his parent had not been a worthless fellow, that, on the contrary, he had been an educated man, a poet and a musician who had brought beauty and wonder into their lives. He had been fond of drinking, yes, but he had died as an artist. In the end, the three men drink a toast with the grateful son to the memory of the father.

The play has two important features. It is written with a poetic sensitivity that Fitzgerald had probably acquired from reading François Villon and others of the decadent romantics. The discovery that a poetic tone can be used to refine and heighten the effect of prose was the single most important step in the development of Fitzgerald's narrative art during the first stage of his career at Princeton. Also significant is the likelihood that the source for the story came from deep within the author himself. Fitzgerald had always considered his father a failure, which, by objective standards, he was. But he had taught his son to read and write and had told him many fantastic and wonderful stories which had stimulated the boy's imagination.

In "Shadow Laurels" Fitzgerald seems to be reaching down into his private feelings for the first time to grasp a subject for his prose. Since we know he was being exposed to the traditionally enlightening college experience of having old ideas and faiths brought into doubt, it seems probable that he used the story as a means of reevaluating the degree of his indebtedness to his father.

The June 1915 issue of the *Nassau Lit* carried his next story, "The Ordeal." This is an account of the mystical occurrence experienced by a young man at the moment he takes his vows for priesthood. The story is strangely vague and inconclusive. It would seem to reflect Fitzgerald's unsettled feeling regarding his Catholicism. Since Newman days, he had been greatly influenced by his friend and advisor, Sigourney Fay. In fact, Father Fay and Shane Leslie together "had induced Fitzgerald to believe he was the future Catholic novelist for the United States."[4] While this ambition was not realized, Fitzgerald nonetheless was able to deal more meaningfully with the theme of religious experience in subsequent stories—of which "Absolution" is perhaps the best example.

"The Ordeal" is the last significant prose piece published by Fitzgerald for nearly a year and a half. His grades during his sophomore year were not good, and he found himself obliged once again to submit to reexamination in the fall. The deficiencies were not satisfactorily made up. So it was that in November of 1915, now in poor health, he withdrew from school. That year's Triangle show, *The Evil Eye,* with book written by Edmund Wilson, again carried seventeen lyrics by Fitzgerald. But the bitterly disappointed student had been forcibly removed from what he always felt was his rightful place in the spotlight. The experience of marking time while his class moved ahead was one which affected him deeply. When he returned to Princeton in September of 1916 he was, in many ways, a different person.

IV

The 1916–1917 Triangle show was called *Safety First,* and for it Fitzgerald produced twenty-one lyrics. This was the third

---

[4] Shane Leslie, "Scott Fitzgerald's First Novel": *The Times Literary Supplement,* November 6, 1959, p. 643.

operetta for which he had provided the songs, and one observes that he had now developed and perfected his natural facility for versifying to a point where some of his best lyrics possessed genuine wit and polish. Included in the *Safety First* score is the following bright verse about Charlotte Corday:

> Back where Robespiere [sic] ruled
> In frivolous fickle France
> That's when someone was fooled
> And fooled in a bold way
> Fooled in the old way.
> Young Miss Charlotte Corday
> Of the "Follies of Ninety Three"
> Asked old Marat to buy her a hat
> Oh mercy on me!
> So Marat he had it sent
> And to her flat he went. Oh:
> Chorus: Charlotte Corday, Charlotte Corday,
> You had them all on the string.
> Gee they were mean to guillotine
> A sweet little innocent thing!
> Got the hat when you wanted it,
> Tried it on but it didn't fit.
> Then you joined the wrath club,
> Stabbed him in the bathtub.
> Served him just right, he was a fright,
> You were impetuous through life.
> Many a dame does just the same,
> But stabs with her eyes, not a knife.
> Still, we've thought upon it
> And we wear your bonnet,
> Charlotte Corday, Charlotte Corday,
> You were some girl in your day!

It was a more sober young man, however, who wrote these songs. After January of 1917, the amount of humorous material that Fitzgerald published gradually declined. (He had been in earlier years a frequent contributor to the Princeton humor magazine, *The Tiger;* but his *Tiger* pieces had always been slight and—he must have realized this—inconsequential.) It appears that it was during his period of readjustment at Princeton that Fitzgerald's humor was transformed into the irony that pervades so much of his subsequent work.

With the frivolity and gaiety of the Triangle show behind him, it was the *Nassau Lit* that then assumed greatest importance as a means for making his creative talents known. Between January and October of 1917, the magazine published six of his short stories and five poems. Included in this production are the best prose pieces that he wrote prior to the publication of *This Side of Paradise*. This is explained in part by the fact that by late fall his romance with Ginevra King had come to a moment of crisis. When the new year began, Fitzgerald had to face the painful truth that their relationship was for all purposes ended. In the manner of "Shadow Laurels," he now used his stories as means of coming to grips with and attempting to understand his past experience. "The Debutante," published in the January 1917 issue, is an episode in play form which depicts a bored, fickle, pseudo-sophisticated young society girl in the process of driving one of her ardent beaux to despair. It is a brief little sketch, but Fitzgerald fully understood the impression he wanted to convey and he conveyed it effectively. In the February issue appeared his story "The Spire and the Gargoyle." He had written it originally in the midst of his depression, while he was waiting to return to school. It concerns a boy who has collected fifty cuts in his spring term and finds himself obliged to take an exam that will determine whether he will be able to return in the fall as a sophomore. The "spire" is the romantic symbol of university existence (which ideally has no imposed disciplines); the "gargoyle" represents the instructor who grades the boy's paper and mercilessly fails him. The second half of the story expresses Fitzgerald's sense of despair over the injustice of a dull, plodding pedagogue (who subsequently takes a job teaching in a high school) having in his hands the power to destroy the plans of a bright, ambitious, gifted young man. It remains a moving and eloquent expression of Fitzgerald's disillusionment at that time.

The April issue carried his "plotted" story "Tarquin of Cheapside," which is structurally similar to his St. Paul Academy piece, "The Room with the Green Blinds." Both stories build to a melodramatic surprise ending. "Tarquin," however, is a far superior narrative in that Fitzgerald's cultivation of poetry had enabled him to produce a carefully controlled poetic prose that is actually the story's outstanding feature. In May, having reconsidered his experience with Ginevra King, he published "Babes in the Woods," a story about two young people feeling each other out in the early stages of their romance. It is a more effective story than "The Debutante," partly because it probes deeper into the author's feelings for its emotional tension. Fitzgerald now understood his two young people (Isabelle and Kenneth) quite well. These two stories, in revised form, figure in *This Side of Paradise*. Isabelle, incidentally, remains as the name of the book's early heroine, and Kenneth becomes Amory. Both stories were sold in 1919 to the *Smart Set* before *Paradise* was accepted for publication.

In June the *Lit* published Fitzgerald's "Sentiment—and the Use of Rouge," a war-time story set in England, full of literary allusions and "big" questions. It is the least successful story of this late period for it clearly reveals Fitzgerald to be, in philosophical matters, a decidely immature thinker. (However, readers of his first two novels will perceive that he was not one to give up without a fight.) The last story Fitzgerald published in the *Lit* was "The Pierian Spring and the Last Straw," which appeared in the October issue. In it the narrator's uncle tells of a sad love affair which we recognize as a new version of the Ginevra King experience. Time has now separated the author from his days of apprehension and ultimate sorrow, and we observe "Fitzgerald the writer" reviewing an incident from the life of "Fitzgerald the boy from St. Paul" and molding the fundamental emotions into a well-fashioned literary creation.

The twenty-one-year-old Princeton student had now acquired all of the individual writer's tools that he would use in his first novel. His material had been determined, his style had been set, his artistic sensitivities had been awakened and sharpened. Most significantly, he had begun to live *actively,* conscious of his time. He would borrow other ideas and he would adapt other styles; but henceforth all of these would be measured against his acquired sense of what was esthetically correct and desirable.

V

In November of 1917, the month after the publication of "The Pierian Spring," the young writer left Princeton to accept a commission in the U.S. Army as a second lieutenant. Fitzgerald's life as a student had come to an end. However, before he left Princeton, he brought to Dean Christian Gauss, his friend, the manuscript of a novel on which he had been working—in the hope that Gauss would recommend it to a publisher. He had titled it *The Romantic Egoist* and had filled its pages with his personal experiences and his youthful philosophy. This was the first draft of the novel that would eventually form part of *This Side of Paradise*. Dean Gauss found it to be unmarketable and advised Fitzgerald to do more work on it. The writer believed in the book and took it with him when he left Princeton to report for duty. What happened to him and his manuscript in the next two years properly belongs to the study of his first novel. In reality, of course, the break between these two early stages of Fitzgerald's life was not distinct or abrupt. In a sense, the "school" and the "young novelist" periods merge into and reflect one another. Fitzgerald came to be in the "outside world" the image of what he had been during his school years, but magnified because of society's larger perspective. In his writing, too, the close interrelationship is implicit. It is true, as many have pointed out, that *This Side of Paradise,* being so unmistakably autobiographical, clearly depicts the life of the young writer. But it is also true that, when considered in detail, Fitzgerald's early writings explain and illuminate the novel called *This Side of Paradise.*

Sy Kahn

This Side of Paradise:
The Pageantry of Disillusion

In his first novel, *This Side of Paradise,* published in 1920 when the author was twenty-three years old, F. Scott Fitzgerald announced the major themes of his total work. The novel reveals that Fitzgerald had an early grasp of his essential material although he had not yet learned to exploit it expertly. In some ways his first novel is the most instructive of his four completed novels; here he nakedly and naïvely exposed his themes before his increased sophistication shaped his insights into the more impressive configurations of *The Great Gatsby* (1925) and *Tender Is the Night* (1934). In Amory Blaine, hero of *This Side of Paradise,* we can see the child who is father to the later men, and in his dilemmas we find the compelling themes of Fitzgerald's work.

All of Fitzgerald's heroes, his "brothers" as he called them, from Amory Blaine to Dick Diver, were men concerned with fashioning a code or sustaining a belief, and, most important, all feel the restraints of the American Puritan heritage. Like Nick Carraway, the narrator in *The Great Gatsby,* they are men full of "interior rules" whose sources lie in the moral codes of American life previous to World War I. Despite the impact of the first World War on sexual mores and drinking, and the fact that, according to Amory, "four men have discovered Paris to one that discovered God," he remains a conscience- and guilt-ridden character. Fitzgerald said of himself that his was a New England conscience raised in Minnesota; Midwest-born, Minnesota-raised

Reprinted from The Midwest Quarterly, *VII (January 1966), 177–194, by permission of the publisher.*

Amory is Fitzgerald's fictional counterpart. "Now a confession will have to be made," wrote Fitzgerald early in *This Side of Paradise,* "Amory had rather a Puritan conscience. Not that he yielded to it—later in life he nearly completely slew it—but at fifteen it made him consider himself a great deal worse than other boys. . . ." The important word here is "nearly," both for Amory and for Fitzgerald himself. There is no evidence in the novel that Amory triumphed over, much less slew, his Puritan conscience. Indeed, it is that very conscience that shapes his imagination and his vision of reality and prepares him for a series of disillusionments.

As its title suggests, *This Side of Paradise* is something of an allegory in which American Youth is caught between the forces of Good and Evil. Among Americans, and especially among the young, "morality" and "sex" are interchangeable terms. Frequently the judgment of "right" and "wrong" behavior rests almost exclusively on sexual behavior. Evil is identified with sex: there the devil wields his greatest powers. If Dante were a young American, Francesca and Paolo might sit at the right hand of Satan. On a number of occasions Amory finds himself caught between his Puritan distrust of sex and the body and the relaxed social and sexual rituals of his time. Like many of his readers, Amory idealized women but found it difficult to maintain his ennobled feelings when they were tested by flesh and blood, the frequent dilemma of the Puritan conscience and a theme much employed in American literature ever since Hawthorne explored it. Amory's ambivalence is dramatized early in the novel when he goes to a party and finds himself alone with Myra and on the verge of his first kiss.

> Sudden revulsion seized Amory, disgust, loathing for the whole incident. He desired frantically to be away, never to see Myra again, never to kiss anyone; he became conscious of his face and hers, of their clinging hands, and he wanted to creep out of his body and hide somewhere safe out of sight, up in the corner of his mind.
> "Kiss me again." Her voice came out of a great void.
> "I don't want to," he heard himself saying. There was another pause.
> "I don't want to!" he repeated passionately.

Many critics have noted that *This Side of Paradise* seems odd to us now as a novel of "flaming youth," and that its scenes of moral laxness and dissipation are today's innocent conventions. It may never have been the revelation of youthful manners, however, that accounted for the book's popularity; it may well have been Fitzgerald's manipulation of the puritanical Amory Blaine that wrenched the conscience of his readers and dramatized their own youthful dilemmas in much the same way as Salinger's Holden Caulfield speaks for the questing youth of the 1950's and 60's.

Amory's early skirmishes with girls anticipate his later engagement with women and the full battle of the sexes. During his Princeton days he carries on a romantic and sentimental correspondence with Isabelle Borgé. During a weekend at Isabelle's home, however, Amory discovers that it is not the girl but his egoistic image of himself as conquering lover that has enchanted him, and the romance is punctured as easily as he bruises her neck with his shirt stud when he embraces her. Her simple and fleshly "ouch" punctuates the college romance, and the spat that follows makes Amory aware that "he had not an ounce of real affection for Isabelle." This comic interlude further dramatizes the difference between woman as romantic illusion and woman as reality, but the theme is lightly touched here. Isabelle was never flesh or woman enough to impel the deeper dilemmas of Amory Blaine.

Not long before the conclusion of his college romance a more instructive incident occurs in Amory's life which announces a theme that Fitzgerald will combine with the themes of sex and evil to complicate the vision of his hero. Returning to Princeton by car, Amory and his friends discover that another carload of students has overturned and killed Dick Humbird, one of the promising men of Princeton. The sudden shock of Humbird's death unnerves and penetrates Amory deeper than he can know. Here is the first victim of many scenes of violence and death in Fitzgerald's novels, bizarre and surrealistic scenes which he depicted with unusual skill and which always carry a heavy burden of meaning. Humbird's death is announced by a spectral "old crone" whose cracked, hollow voice and flapping kimono complete the image of a night-riding harpy. Oracularly she points to the corpse lying under a roadside arc-light, face down in a widening circle of blood. The night wind stirs a broken fender "to a plaintive tinny sound." In this novel, set in the years during and immediately after World War I, Fitzgerald calls the roll of Amory's dead classmates, beginning with Humbird, just as he continued to count the dead of his generation all his life. The event marks a transition in Amory; it breaks his illusion that youth is permanent and indestructible.

Some weeks after Humbird's death, Amory and his college friend Fred Sloan escort two chorus girls during an evening in New

York. The events of this evening lay open for us the tortured heart and mind of the youngest of Fitzgerald's "brothers." Now Amory must face the full reality of women as sexual creatures, neither glamorized nor sentimentalized. The two couples go to a cafe where Amory is aware of being watched by a middle-aged, faintly smiling man in a brown sack suit. Then, Amory and the others go to upper Manhattan where the girls have an apartment among the "tall, white-stone buildings, dotted with dark windows" that stretch endlessly, "flooded with bright moonlight that gave them a calcium pallor." From the moment that the mysterious, pale-faced man had scrutinized Amory, the party develops a sensual and evil atmosphere. The white buildings and the moonlight recall the arc-light which spotlighted Humbird's death and anticipate the spectral appearance of the ominous man in the apartment. While Amory sat on the sofa with Axia, "There was a minute while temptation crept over him like a warm wind, and his imagination turned to fire. . . ." At that instant he is astonished to discover the man who had been in the cafe: "There the man sat, half leaned against a pile of pillows in the corner of the divan. His face was cast in the same yellow wax as in the cafe, neither the dull, pasty color of a dead man—rather a sort of virile pallor—nor unhealthy. . . ."

This image of the devil is the symbol of shock, born of the impact of sensuality upon Puritan morality, conscience, and Catholic sense of sin. The most shocking detail about the man is his feet, which are encased in moccasins, "pointed, though, like the shoes they wore in the fourteenth century, and with the little ends curling up." It is "unutterably terrible" that the toes seem to fill them to the end. First Amory is transfixed by this vision of evil; then he bolts. Fitzgerald continues to build Amory's terror by carefully patterning the images of pale light throughout the successive scenes, images that connect these events with Humbird's death scene. Down the long streets of New York shines the moonlight, palely reflected from the white buildings. He is horrified to realize that he is not fleeing the strange footsteps but following them, setting, as it were, his own foot on the path to hell:

> . . . he turned off the street and darted into an alley, narrow and dark and smelling of old rottenness. He twisted down a long, sinuous blackness, where the moonlight was shut away except for the tiny glints and patches . . . then suddenly sank panting into a corner by a fence, exhausted.

Thus Amory escapes, in fact, his sexual encounter with Axia,

haunted as he is by a man whose face is a pallid mask reminiscent
of Humbird and of the devil himself. But his flight down moon-
drenched streets leads him to an alley whose sexual symbolism
makes him psychologically experience what he has physically
avoided.

No Goodman Brown ever emerged from his bewitched forest
more haunted and guilt-ridden than young Amory from the stone
jungle of twentieth-century New York. On the streets of the city
he seems caught up in an interior morality play that obliterates his
surroundings. As he walks, praying for someone "stupid" and
"good" to save him, he hears something clang "like a low gong
struck at a distance," and again, by this device, we are reminded
of the torn fender of Humbird's death car banging in the wind.
Then before Amory's eyes: "a face flashed over the two feet, a
face pale and distorted with a sort of infinite evil that twisted it
like a flame in the wind; *but he knew, for the half instant that the
gong twanged and hummed, that it was the face of Dick Humbird*
[Fitzgerald's italics]." By means of the device of light and sound
imagery, Fitzgerald associates the devil with the face of the dead
classmate and creates a vision in which the major themes of sex,
evil, and death meet to shape the face and figure of the devil.

For the rest of this momentous weekend Amory reverberates
to his encounter with temptation and evil. The painted faces of
Broadway make him ill, and he rails at Sloan that New York is
"ghastly" and "filthy" while Sloan wonders what would have happened if Amory had "gone through with our little party." He abandons Sloan for a purgative "head massage" in a barber shop, but
"the smell of the powders and tonics brought back Axia's sidelong,
suggestive smile, and he left hurriedly." On the train for Princeton
a "painted woman" brings on a new wave of nausea and he changes
cars, until finally, back at Princeton, on a wild and windy night,
he joins his friend Tom. As the young men settle down to try to
study, and the "wet branches moved and clawed with their finger-
nails on the window pane," both of them are suddenly electrified
by a sense of the presence of evil. Tom thinks he sees the flash of
a face at the window. "Something was looking at you," he tells
Amory, and Amory, unnerved, replies, "I've had one hell of an
experience. I think I've seen the devil or—something like him."

If the white buildings of New York, blanched by the moon,
are the symbols of evil, the gothic spires of Princeton are the
architecture of sanity and safety. Early in the novel Fitzgerald
establishes this contrast when he tells us that through the shell

of Amory's undergraduate consciousness "had broken a deep and reverent devotion to the gray walls and Gothic peaks and all they symbolized as warehouses of dead ages." Consequently, when Amory returns to the college after his encounter with "the devil" in New York, "he nearly cried aloud with joy when the towers of Princeton loomed up beside him and the yellow squares of light filtered through the blue rain." Here there is no phallic thrust of dark-windowed, pale buildings, but rather the steady lights, green spaces, and chaste spires of sanctuary. For Amory Blaine, transplanted from Minnesota to Princeton, the University is his stronghold, the monastic fortress for his Catholic-Puritan conscience this side of Paradise.

During the last years of his college life, Amory's encounter with sensuality provides a "sombre background . . . that filled his nights with a dreary terror and made him unable to pray." An indifferent Catholic, he is, nevertheless, almost as much disturbed by the "ghost of a code," this "gaudy, ritualistic, paradoxical Catholicism," as he is by the specters born of his puritanical conscience. In America, Leslie Fiedler has pointed out, "The sensibility of the Catholic . . . becomes like everything else puritan." Amory illustrates the point early in the novel when he derides the easy kiss, the hip flask, the petting interlude in parked cars even though he tries to play the role of the alert and conforming adolescent of his time. Following his encounter with death and the devil, in the interlude before his graduation and participation in the war, Amory does find in Clara Page, a distant cousin, a woman he can idealize. Monsignor Thayer Darcy, family friend and confidant, urges Amory to seek her out in Philadelphia. He discovers in Clara a woman in whom sex has been translated into intelligence and vitality. She is blonde and saintly, husbandless but with babies to care for; in short, she is the Madonna figure that permits the man haunted by puritanical notions of sexual evil to release his ardor in pure and exalted feeling. Clara is Beatrice to his incipient Dante. Images of light accumulate about her blonde head, haloed and hallowed as she is by young Amory's romantic idealism. "She was immemorial," we are told immediately about her, and too good for any man. Gradually he falls in love with her, or, more rightly, with his own ideal of what women should be, creatures of light, as her name suggests, intelligence and charm, but essentially untouchable. He is entranced with her at church when "she knelt and bent her golden hair into the stained-glass light." Spontaneously and to their mutual embarrassment he calls "St. Cecelia" and confesses that "if I lost faith in you I'd lose faith in God." She reveals to him that she has never been in love, which, of course, brightens the halo about her: "she seemed suddenly a daughter of light alone." Clara remains unsullied and sanctified. Amory realizes she could have been a "devil" if God had bent her soul a little the other way. As Fitzgerald's novels reveal, Madonnas with "bent souls" are the inevitable partners for Fitzgerald's tormented brethren, his "spoiled priests."

After Amory graduates he goes to France to fight, but Fitzgerald telescopes the years 1917 and 1918 by the device of quoting several letters. He misses the opportunity here of deepening the history of Amory's disillusion because he could not construct incidents for Amory from a world he himself did not know. Indeed Fitzgerald served in the army, but he was never sent abroad. The metaphor of war was not natural to him, not a part of his vision or disillusioning experience as it was for his contemporary, Ernest Hemingway. Consequently, when next we truly confront Amory, it is in post-war New York, and with no sense that he is a veteran, and the clear notion that he is still a virgin. It is in the battle of the sexes rather than in the trenches that Amory receives his sudden and lasting wounds.

In his engagement to Rosalind Connage, the post-war debutante-flapper, Amory suffers painful disillusionment. The trauma of her eventual rejection of him is the first expression of a situation that haunts Fitzgerald's total work with nightmarish regularity. It is probable that the source of Fitzgerald's obsessive concern with losing the girl one loves was in his fear of losing his fiancée Zelda Sayre because he had neither the position nor money to support her. In Amory Blaine's loss of Rosalind, for these very reasons he plays out a drama that might have been his own. In his work there are many variations on the nightmare: Gatsby and Daisy, Diver and Nicole, to state the most obvious examples. The wealthy Rosalind breaks her engagement with Amory because his meager job in an advertising agency cannot hope to support her in any style. "You'd hate me in a narrow atmosphere. I'd make you hate me," she tells him. It is the recognition of this hard, economic fact that eventually turns Amory toward socialism at the end of the novel. "I'm sick of a system," he says then, "where the richest man gets the most beautiful girl if he wants her. . . ." Fitzgerald never underestimated the fact that love and economics are intertwined in human affairs, and that when the forces of love and wealth are pitted against each other, wealth often strips love of its sentimentalities and illusions. There is not a single hero in his novels who is not, one way or another, undone by the power and strategies of wealth. Amory is the first of Fitzgerald's innocent Adams disemboweled by savage Eves.

In the despair of his disillusion he discovers that New York, which once gave him a vision of the devil, now offers him a variety of dissipations: drunkenness, half-remembered encounters in night clubs, and finally a severe beating. In Fitzgerald's novels his heroes take beatings at those points when they are emotionally bankrupt. These manifest the psychic wounding that has taken place and symbolize as well the desire for punishment for having lost one's moral grip. One remembers Anthony Patch of *The Beautiful and Damned* beaten up on a New York street, and Dick Diver mauled by taxi drivers after his sexual capitulation to Rosemary in Rome, both men at the nadir of their disillusionment and at their lowest emotional ebb. As for Jay Gatsby, he is shot to death and thus saved at the last moment from complete disillusionment about Daisy, as if only death could keep a Fitzgerald man from the inevitable knowledge of the failed female.

Having painfully learned that attractiveness and intelligence are not adequate substitutes for wealth, Amory retreats to Washington to visit Thayer Darcy, but missing connections, he decides to recuperate with an ancient uncle in Maryland. In the fields of Ramilly County he meets nineteen-year-old Eleanor Savage, whom he finds one stormy night perched atop a haystack reciting Verlaine while rain pours and lightning cracks. Her last name, the lightning flashes, as when Tom saw the devil looking at Amory, and Amory's opening address to her inform us that the young man is about to encounter evil again. "Who the devil is there in Ramilly County . . . who would deliver Verlaine in an extemporaneous tune to a soaking haystack?" he asks. When she inquires who he is, he replies "I'm Don Juan," and the new romance commences. The wild landscape of Maryland, "the half-sensual, half-neurotic quality of this autumn with Eleanor," insure that Amory is about to pass another season in hell. To Maryland both bring small histories of youthful disillusionment. If Amory has seen Rosalind unmask the face of love to reveal the tight-lipped face of wealth, Eleanor has discovered that the romantic mask hides the leering face of sex. For three weeks they take various poses with each other, until one moonlit night when they seemed "dim phantasmal shapes, expressing eternal beauty in curious elfin moods," they symbolically turn out of the moonlight into the "trellised darkness

of a vine-hung pagoda," and he catches her in his arms. In a eu-
phemistic passage, Fitzgerald suggests that Amory has at last been
sexually initiated, but the "novel of flaming youth" is not so
graphic or direct as to make this certain: "'you are mine—you
know you're mine!' he cried wildly . . . the moonlight twisted in
through the vines and listened . . . the fireflies hung upon their
whispers as if to win his glance from the glory of their eyes."

Following this ambiguous encounter, on this last night of
Amory's vacation in Maryland, they take their horses for a "farewell trot by the cold moonlight." Angry at the world which forces
her to subordinate her intelligence to less clever men in order to
attract them, angry at a world that will not sustain romantic
illusions, angry at moons that turn cold and clear, she rails, "Oh,
just one person in fifty has any glimmer of what sex is. I'm hipped
on Freud and all that, but it's rotten that every bit of real love in
the world is ninety-nine percent passion and one little soupçon of
jealousy." Amory is quick to agree that sex is "a rather unpleasant
overpowering force that's part of the machinery under everything.
It's like an actor that lets you see his mechanics!"

Now Amory comes fully to grips with the idea that torments
him and abuses his idealism, and in the following passage speaks
for his postwar generation poised on the edge of the decade that
is to reveal many changes in American attitudes:

> You see everyone's got to have some cloak to throw around it. The
> mediocre intellects, Plato's second class, use the remnants of roman-
> tic chivalry diluted with Victorian sentiment—and we who consider
> ourselves the intellectuals cover it by pretending that it's another side
> of us, has nothing to do with our shining brains; we pretend that the
> fact that we realize it is really absolving us from being a prey to it. But
> the truth is that sex is right in the middle of our purest abstractions, so
> close that it obscures vision.

Whatever images of romantic love they had attempted to create
together lie shattered about them; the touch of flesh explodes their
illusions. Relentlessly Amory advances his argument: there is no
protection against sex, neither intellect nor conversation; nor the
Catholic church, counters Eleanor, which shakes him:

> Thousands of scowling priests keeping the degenerate Italians and
> illiterate Irish repentant with gabble-gabble about the sixth and ninth
> commandments. It's just all cloaks, sentiment and spiritual rouge and

panaceas. I tell you there *is* no God, not even a definite abstract goodness; so it's all got to be worked out for the individual by the individual here in the high white foreheads like mine, and you're too much the prig to admit it.

To Amory this is blasphemy, an evil he cannot reconcile with some hard, inner core of values, perhaps his Irish-American puritanism. Eleanor, in a paroxysm of outrage at her discovery of the endless masquerades of sex, turns her horse toward a dark cliff in a suicide attempt. At the last moment she throws herself off the horse while it goes whinnying over the edge. Neither of these babes in the wood is old enough to sustain feeling for the other without romantic illusion, though they are able, some years later, to exchange melancholy poems. In retrospect he realizes that under that high-riding "evil moon" they could "see the devil in each other," and the old puritanical notion that beauty is often the mask for evil fixes itself in his soul.

There remain several more crucial incidents in the novel to complete the pageantry of Amory Blaine's disillusion. Alone in Atlantic City he meets Alec Connage, Rosalind's brother, accompanied by two women, and Amory becomes involved in Alec's sexual intrigue. They catch him up in a distressed moment when he is recalling the gaiety of Princeton escapades, innocent and boisterous, on these same boardwalks and beaches, and now, a few years later, so many of his classmates are already dead. His youth seems vanished and he vaguely longs for death; his listlessness and disillusion are deepened by the thought that women can only hold men by appealing to the worst in them, the "thesis of most of his bad nights."

Agreeing to occupy a hotel room connecting with Alec's, to substitute for a friend of Alec's who needed to leave, Amory goes to the room, mourning the lost Rosalind, and falls asleep while an ominous moon sears the sky. He is awakened by a house detective pounding on Alec's door and the frightened voices of Alec and Jill, a "gaudy, vermillion-lipped blonde," coming from the connecting bathroom. In a terrified moment Alec explains that he cannot lie that Jill is his wife since the house detective knows her, and that he will be liable under the Mann Act; meanwhile the miserable Jill retreats to Amory's bed. At this point Fitzgerald again lifts this scene by the device of surrealistic detail to a level that clearly exposes the themes of the novel:

> Amory realized there were other things in the room besides people
> . . . over and around the figure crouched in the bed, there hung an
> aura, gossamer as a moonbeam, tainted as a stale, weak wine, yet a
> horror, diffusively brooding already over the three of them . . . and
> over by the window among the stirring curtains stood something else,
> featureless and indistinguishable, yet strangely familiar.

Caught between these two evil presences in his room, he swiftly decides to take responsibility for Jill, to take the blame off Alec,
and at that instant the specters near the bed and window vanish. In
that listening, suspended moment evil forms the spectral shapes of
sex and death. For shortly after this incident, in a short scene at the
police station, Amory learns that Monsignor Darcy has died, and
he knows that it was his ghost that stirred the curtains of the hotel
bedroom.

Later, back in New York, in a dreary, rainy autumn, Amory
continues to mourn the lost Rosalind. She has disillusioned him
about love, and her brother has completed the emotional carnage
by the tawdry escapade in Atlantic City. Once again he is sensi-
tized to "the fetid sensuousness of stale powder on women" as he
walks the streets and recoils from the poor of New York whose
poverty seems more vile than it is when sex drives the penniless
men and women together; "it was an atmosphere wherein birth
and marriage and death were loathsome, secret things." The fact
that he is jobless and that his mother has made bad investments,
destroying his private income, makes him all the more fearful and
scornful of the poor as one might shun the worst image of oneself.
Better to be corrupt and rich than innocent and poor, he thinks; it
is essentially cleaner. In the convent of his mind he reviews the
names of his dead loves as a monk might tell the beads of his rosa-
ry: Isabelle, Clara, Rosalind, Eleanor.

Amory's romantic imagination and persistent idealism, rooted
in his Irish-Catholic, Puritan-Midwestern-American background
save him from complete despair. If on the one hand his puritanical
sensibilities operate to prepare him for outrage, frustration, and
disillusionment, especially in his encounters with women, on the
other hand they provide him with a certain armor against *amour.*
The ambiguity is, perhaps, suggested by his name. Fitzgerald im-
plies as well that Amory's romanticism and idealism are mystical
legacies passed on to him by the death of Monsignor Darcy.
Amory's sacrifice of reputation for Alec, and his realization that
Alec will eventually hate him for it bring him "the full realization

of his disillusion, but of Monsignor's funeral was born the romantic elf that was to enter the labyrinth with him." In the later novels, particularly *The Great Gatsby* and *Tender Is the Night,* the romantic idealism of his heroes, elves in the labyrinth, at once insures their inevitable defeat in a world where the labyrinth is more torturous and dangerous, and the emotional and monetary stakes higher. Fitzgerald recognized that real minotaurs make short work of chivalrous and charming elves.

After various shocking disillusionments have knocked Amory's idealism off-balance, he reacts for a time by imagining himself deteriorating in the sweet acid of sensual abandon, a sort of evil heaven where disillusioned Puritans go:

> Port Said, Shanghai, parts of Turkestan, Constantinople, the South Seas—all lands of sad, haunting music and many odors, where lust could be a mode and expression of life, where the shades of night skies and sunsets would seem to reflect only moods of passion: the color of lips and poppies.

He would like to "let himself go to the devil," and "to sink safely and sensuously out of sight." But these thoughts also give rise to a sense of panic and guilt as he wonders if merely thinking such thoughts does not create an evil aura around him that may infect the innocent. He fears he has lost the ability to "scent evil," to ferret out instinctively "the deeper evils in pride and sensuality." The Puritan need to identify and judge evil sobers and steadies him and dispels the colorful specters of sensuality.

> The pageantry of his disillusion took shape in a world-old procession of Prophets, Athenians, Martyrs, Saints, Scientists, Don Juans, Jesuits, Puritans, Fausts, Poets, Pacifists; like costumed alumni at a college reunion they streamed before him as their dreams, personalities, and creeds had in turn thrown colored lights on his soul.

Women had not proved adequate to his imagination; philosophers and political leaders canceled out each other's thoughts; few were the men who were not emotional or intellectual or spiritual cripples. Yet he feels that he has "escaped from a small enclosure into a great labyrinth," and that he will undertake its mysteries, starting all inquiries with himself, chastened by self-reproach, loneliness, and disillusion.

In this mixed mood of regeneration and disillusion, Amory

sets off, like a pilgrim in a more apparent allegory, to walk to Princeton. On a cool, gray day, "that least fleshly of all weathers; a day of dreams and far hopes and clear visions," his sense of the real begins to clarify. "The problem of evil had solidified for Amory into the problem of sex," which comes as no surprise if we have followed his history, and his thought leads him to link evil with beauty. Each time he has reached out for beauty, "it had leered out at him with the grotesque face of evil. Beauty of great art, beauty of all joy, most of all the beauty of women." To his mind beauty has too many associations with license and indulgence and weakness, and weak things are never good. Before he reaches Princeton, he stops at twilight in an old graveyard, a scene symbolically appropriate to a purging of the past and to these phoenix-like moments of transition. If certain illusions are to be buried there, certain revelations have given him new strength. The graves do not convince him that life is vain; "Somehow he could find nothing hopeless in having lived."

After midnight Amory arrives at Princeton and once again finds in the towers and spires and late-burning lights the fit symbols of his hopes. No ominous white buildings here, no evil moon. The novitiates must learn to bear the shock of exploding illusions, must grow up to find "all Gods dead, all wars fought, all faiths in man shaken." He feels sorry for them but not for himself; he is safe and free now, to "accept what was acceptable, roam, grow, rebel." Thus at the end of the novel, in a gesture more richly ambiguous of both acceptance and crucifixion than perhaps Fitzgerald could know at twenty-three, Amory "stretched out his arms to the crystalline, radiant sky" and announces, "I know myself . . . but that is all."

Fitzgerald's first novel reveals a number of observations that were to become persistent themes in his later work. The young Amory wants above all else to have popularity and power. Later he discovers that it is not admiration he wants, or even love, "but to be necessary to people, to be indispensable," and to give them "a sense of security." These "immense desires" are also manifest in Gatsby and even more dramatically revealed in Dick Diver. Furthermore, Fitzgerald's description of Rosalind announces a catalog of ideas thematically developed in his subsequent work. "Her fresh enthusiasm, her will to grow and learn, her endless faith in the inexhaustibility of romance, her courage and her fundamental honesty—these things were not spoiled." Spoiled, however, they are doomed to be, and it is in the loss of these qualities in his characters that we sense the pathos of their defeat. Fitzgerald called evil the forces that brought about these failures. When Monsignor Darcy writes of Amory that he has "that half-miraculous sixth sense" by which he detects evil, "the half-realized fear of God" in his heart, the lines reveal the author as tellingly as they do Amory Blaine. Taken as a whole, Fitzgerald's fiction testifies to his talent for identifying the corruption and moral failure masked by the surface glitter and carnival antics of the 1920's. His concern with evil, as he understood it, is everywhere apparent in his work, and his desire to reveal it prompted him to write in *This Side of Paradise:* "Every author ought to write every book as if he were going to be beheaded the day he finished it."

Under the edict of this urgent credo, Fitzgerald created heroes who were clearly projections of himself, and these "brothers" must confront the disillusionments that instruct them and sometimes break and kill them. They are brothers in another sense, too, in that they are related to each other by thematic blood lines. His heroes are variously undone by an idealism bravely asserted but doomed. Amory, it is true, unlike his elder "brothers," survives his disillusioning experiences by virtue of his resilient youth and his sense of flexing and stretching a new, marvelous self, but one cannot help imagining, especially in the light of the novels that followed, that his judgments concerning sex and beauty will doom him, will drive him into a corner, much as Dick Diver fades away into Upper New York after his fall in Italy and France. The final image of Amory, opening his arms to receive the limitless universe, becomes, from another angle of vision, the dead Gatsby floating in his pool, or a broken Dick Diver making an ironic sign of the cross over the beach on the Riviera. Yet Amory Blaine, Jay Gatsby, and Dick Diver are meant to win our sympathy because they cling to a romantic, Platonic image of themselves in spite of their disillusioning pilgrimages. There is no doubt that Fitzgerald intended these heroes to be nobler and more humane in their defeat than the people and forces that undo them. The elder heroes hang crucified upon the crosses of their idealism, defeated yet elevated above the men and women who have nailed them there. They have walked a terrain where certain events disarm and disillusion them, but Fitzgerald's craft insures that his heroes remain the brightest points in the landscape.

Sergio Perosa

The Beautiful and Damned

The theme of *The Beautiful and Damned*—published serially in *The Metropolitan Magazine* (September 1921–March 1922) before being issued in book form—is the dissipation and deterioration of the inner self. Two people, husband and wife, are equally guilty of an excessive indulgence in illusions and dreams. This idea of a motivated failure of the protagonists was in the author's mind since the very first conception of the new novel, even if he was thinking at the time of giving a new portrait of the young aesthete:

> My new novel [he had written in 1920] called *The Flight of the Rocket,* concerns the life of one Anthony Patch between his 25th and 33d years (1913–1921). He is one of those many with the tastes and weaknesses of an artist but with no actual creative inspiration. How he and his beautiful young wife are wrecked on the shoals of dissipation is told in the story. (*Letters,* Turnbull, ed., [New York, 1963], p. 145.)

If ties with the "young artist" that Amory had been are still visible, we cannot say that the new novel was to continue his story, because Anthony Patch is bound from the start to become a failure, and his story is to be seen in close interdependence with the story of his wife. The interdependence of the two characters was emphasized in the title of the manuscript, which was called "The Beautiful Lady Without Mercy" and had furthermore an epigraph taken from Keats's "La Belle Dame Sans

From The Art of F. Scott Fitzgerald *by Sergio Perosa. Copyright, the University of Michigan Press, 1965. Reprinted by permission of the publisher.*

Merci."[1] This epigraph disappeared in the published version of the novel—the new title clearly indicating that both Anthony and Gloria were victims of a romantic conception of the world. But the main theme of the dissipation of the two characters remained as it had been conceived originally, all the more painful because their ruin is the result of an apparent, but deceptive material victory. Anthony and Gloria struggle against philistinism and hypocritical morality so as to be able to prolong their dissipation, but their victory, reached when it is too late, only serves to make the feeling of incurable defeat the more terrible. "The victor belongs to the spoils," reads the new epigraph: and there was never a more bitter and hollow victory than this one, which leaves the two characters among the spoils and remnants of their struggle and of their existence. It is a pathetic struggle, too weakly and too selfishly fought to become tragic, which reveals the flaws of decay and deterioration under the golden appearance of success. As with Amory in the earlier novel, the story of the two characters, so "beautiful and damned," is developed as a moral parable, linearly unfolded, though with a better feeling for the general structure. And the parable is precisely that of the youthful dreams and illusions that gradually become a lethargy and then a nightmare and are involved in an inevitable ruin.

The novel is divided into three books,[2] each in turn divided into three chapters. Each book represents a distinct moment in the development of the story, while the chapters themselves mark the progressive unfolding of the parable. From a complete abandonment to dreams at the beginning, the two protagonists fall to tasting the lees of an illusory happiness and find that the dreams have become nightmares. Just as in *This Side of Paradise,* a "portrait" of Anthony is given at the very beginning: he is a sophisticated and blasé aesthete, who lives in a comfortable ivory tower in a New York apartment. More mature than Amory and lacking his sentimental obsession with socialism, Anthony has the advantage of a certain culture (he reads Flaubert's *Education Sentimentale* . . .), is independent and rich and has his future assured by the prospect of a big inheritance. He is more refined

---

[1] In the MS there is also an epigraph from Samuel Butler: "Life is a long process of getting tired," which was not used in the printed text.

[2] In the MS the three books bear these titles: "The Pleasant Absurdity of Things," "The Romantic Bitterness of Things," and "The Ironic Tragedy of Things."

than his predecessor and enjoys the close friendship of a small set
of people, through whom he makes hesitant and timid approaches
to the world. His real desire is to perpetuate his pleasant life; he is
content to contemplate his own image (there is a touch of Narcis-
sus in him, too) in the golden mirrors and polished surfaces of his
house. His favorite retreat is the bathtub, and there he weaves
immaterial dreams, castles in the air, reveries of himself contemplating sensual beauties, or playing imaginary violins:

> He felt that if he had a love he would have hung her picture
> just facing the tub so that, lost in the soothing steamings of the hot
> water, he might lie and look up at her and muse warmly and sensu-
> ously on her beauty. . . . (*BD,* pp. 11–12.)
> He raised his voice to compete with the flood of water pouring
> into the tub, and as he looked at the picture of Hazel Dawn upon
> the wall he put an imaginary violin to his shoulder and softly caressed
> it with a phantom bow. (*BD,* p. 17.)

All his social and cultural attempts dissolve in that dreamy
atmosphere. He feels compelled to do something, and he can
think of nothing better than writing a history of the Middle
Ages. He feels that he should allow himself some diversions, and
he finds a girl, Geraldine, who offers him a new mirror in which
to gaze at himself. She is held at a distance and kept for certain
hours, because "she was company, familiar, and faintly intimate
and restful. Further than that he did not care to experiment
—not from any moral compunction, but from a dread of allowing any entanglement to disturb what he felt was the growing
serenity of his life."

A "Flash-Back in Paradise," however, marking the birth of
the "beautiful" Gloria, is sufficient to put the serenity of his life
in jeopardy. Gloria is a new, more dangerous incarnation of the
"debutante" or flapper, both careless and fascinating. She, too,
is possessed by an illusory dream, the dream of a beauty to
whom all is due, who accepts no responsibility and subordinates
every other aspect of life to an aesthetic principle. To Gloria,
"who took all things of life for hers to choose from and appor-
tion, as though she were continually picking out presents for herself from an inexhaustible counter," it is enough for people to
"fit into the picture." She does not mind "if they don't do anything." "I don't see why they should—in fact it almost astonishes
me when anybody does anything."

Her meeting with Anthony is therefore perfectly logical and

unavoidable. And yet, if the aesthete gives up his dream of detachment from the world, of aloofness and isolation, it is only to replace it with a new dream—the dream of eternal love. He knows very well that he is not "a realist," that Gloria requites his love because he is "clean," but greatly interested as he is by every girl "who made a living directly on her prettiness," there is no possible escape for him. It can be either "white" or "black magic," but Gloria fills him with dissatisfaction, then panic, and finally brings him to the altar.

Anthony and Gloria throw their illusions together, but the dream of one cannot but suffer in contact with that of the other. The illusion of love as an absorbing way of life collides with the ideal that sees marriage as a means of satisfying one's vanity:

> Marriage was created not to be a background but to need one
> —says Gloria—. Mine is going to be outstanding. It can't, shan't
> be the setting—it's going to be the performance, the live, lovely,
> glamorous performance, and the world shall be the scenery. (*BD*,
> p. 147.)

After the precarious "radiant hour" (that opens the second book), Anthony finds his serenity compromised, while Gloria finds herself without the much-coveted security. Her "tremendous nervous tension" contrasts with his utter cowardice. A new dream, that of an expected inheritance, keeps them together. But Adam Patch is not so eager to die, and he disapproves of their fast spending and reckless living. He keeps a close watch on them, while they are unconsciously preparing their ruin. Anthony tries in vain to go on with his book and has a short and fruitless working experience; Gloria plays with the idea of becoming a film actress, but her husband objects to it. His further attempt to write commercial short stories is also a failure.

Their dream becomes gradually an inexcusable form of lethargy, and after their refusal to have a child, this lethargy kills even the illusion of eternal love. "Gloria had lulled Anthony's mind to sleep . . . [she] realized that Anthony had become capable of utter indifference toward her, a temporary indifference, more than half lethargic. . . ." Only a childish vision of future happiness and security stirs them at times from their lethargy:

> That spring, that summer, they had speculated upon future
> happiness—how they were to travel from summer land to summer

land, returning eventually to a gorgeous estate and possible idyllic
children, then entering diplomacy or politics, to accomplish, for a
while, beautiful and important things, until finally as a white-haired
(beautifully, silkily, white-haired) couple they were to loll about in
serene glory, worshipped by the bourgeoisie of the land. . . . These
times were to begin "when we get our money"; it was on such
dreams rather than on any satisfaction with their increasingly ir-
regular, increasingly dissipated life that their hope rested. (*BD*, p.
277.)

Their expectation could not rest on weaker foundations. In
a highly dramatic scene, Adam Patch, the old millionaire, who is
a prohibitionist and a supporter of a Victorian moral code, visits
them at the climax of a drunken party. The blow proves fatal
for him and for the hopes of Anthony and Gloria as well, because they are disinherited.

Then lethargy turns into a nightmare. Even Anthony realizes that he "had been futile in longing to drift and dream; no
one drifted except to maelstroms, no one dreamed without his
dreams becoming fantastic nightmares of indecision and regret."
This realization, however, is only temporary, and the two react
by attaching themselves desperately to the hope of winning back
the inheritance. They have now to contest the will, but their
struggle (related in the third book) is really on two fronts, because
their inner tensions break the remaining ties of love and destroy all
their serenity. Anthony welcomes the diversion offered by the war
and enlists to escape, as it were, his own self and his contradictions,
but even this illusion is wrecked by the ruthless impact of reality.

Stationed in a southern military camp, Anthony ends by
getting himself entangled in a sordid love affair, which is represented as "an inevitable result of his increasing carelessness
about himself. . . . He merely slid into the matter through his
inability to make definite judgments." This same inability is responsible for his breaking bounds to go and see his new girl,
with the inevitable result of being stripped of his rank. Thus,
even his respectability and self-respect are ruined, and he
plunges again into a nightmare of helpless impotence and dissatisfaction. Meanwhile, Gloria, who has recognized the failure
of their love ("That she had not been happy with Anthony for
over a year mattered little"), falls back on the obstinate dream
of her beauty. She flirts with old friends and new acquaintances,
makes a new attempt to go into the movies, which results in
bitter failure, and is unable to come to terms with reality. Not

understanding that circumstances and people change, she reverts to childhood, dreaming of being a child again, of being protected, expecting "to wake in some high, fresh-scented room, alone, and statuesque within and without, as in her virginal and colorful past."

But the present intrudes; it offers only the pale image of an Anthony who, back from the military camp, spends his time in the house turning his back on every human or worldly contact. The aesthetic recluse has become the melancholy hermit of indigence and helplessness. Anthony spends his time wearily reading newspapers in the midst of disorder and filth, and now more than ever he has recourse to the deceptive relief of drinking. He too reverts to the dream of his past youth, and he too discovers that he is unfit for the present. Even his drinking aims at recreating an equivocal atmosphere of dreamy sentimentalism and decadent aestheticism:

> There was a kindliness about intoxication—there was that indescribable gloss and glamor it gave, like the memories of ephemeral and faded evenings. After a few high-balls there was magic in the tall glowing Arabian night of the Bush Terminal Building. . . .
> . . . the fruit of youth or of the grape, the transitory magic of the brief passage from darkness to darkness—the old illusion that truth and beauty were in some way entwined. (*BD*, p. 417.)

Anthony comes to realize that it *is* an illusion, but it is a devastating realization. His psychological balance is broken, and he resorts to pointless violence. He provokes Bloeckman, his former rival, to a fight, and when Dorothy, the southern girl, comes to see him in New York, he suffers a nervous collapse. It is at this point that the news reaches him that he has finally won his suit against the will and that he owns thirty million dollars.

Their dream is realized, but only when it is too late. The slow and inexorable passing of time has made this victory *in extremis* a hollow one. With a touch of dramatic irony, the reversal of fortune overtakes the two characters only when their initial situation has been reversed. Anthony, sophisticated and blasé at the beginning, is now an empty shell who goes to Europe with a doctor at his side. Sparkling Gloria, who used to divide people into clean and unclean, now herself appears "sort of dyed and *unclean*."

If we read the story in this way—disentangling its meaning from the mass of obtrusive material and subsidiary aspects—it becomes clear enough that it is a parable on the deceptiveness of dreams, on the impossibility of evading reality through illusions, and on the painful destructiveness of time. The very evil that wears away the life of the flapper who refuses to grow up, and the life of the "philosopher" who cannot come to grips with reality and experience, is hidden in their youthful dreams, in their careless attitude of defiance toward the world, in their refusal to evaluate and accept the effects of time. Far from being the mouthpiece or the singer of the jazz age, Fitzgerald was its lucid accuser. He was well aware of its equivocal dangers, of its irresponsible attitudes, and he pitilessly exposed its disastrous consequences—even admitting that his denunciation was achieved almost in spite of his own intentions and was brought to light in the novel almost unconsciously.

If the meaning of the story told in *The Beautiful and Damned* must be identified with the gradual denunciation of Anthony's and Gloria's irresponsible progress of deterioration, and with an exposition of their guilty behavior toward themselves and the world, one cannot deny that in many passages Fitzgerald reveals a tendency to bestow on Anthony, if not on Gloria, a kind of moral greatness that contradicts the *objective* development of his adventure. At times Fitzgerald seemed to falter between a desire to show the "heroic" side of Anthony and a willingness to criticize his pointless endeavors. The story itself admits of no other possibility than a bitter denunciation of Anthony and Gloria, because their actions speak for themselves, and there is little doubt as to their purport. But at the very end of the book Anthony is represented in an ambiguous light and almost praised for his refusal "to give in, to submit to mediocrity, to go to work":

> Anthony Patch, sitting near the rail and looking out at the sea, was not thinking of his money [!], for he had seldom in his life been really preoccupied with material vainglory. . . . No—he was concerned with a series of reminiscences, much as a general might look back upon a successful campaign and analyze his victories. He was thinking of the hardships, the insufferable tribulations he had gone through. They had tried to penalize him for the mistakes of his youth. . . .
>
> Only a few months before people had been urging him to give in, to submit to mediocrity, to go to work. But he had known that he was justified in his way of life—and he had stuck it out staunchly. . . .

"I showed them," 'he was saying. "It was a hard fight, but I didn't give up and I came through!" (*BD,* pp. 448–49.)

His last words are words of self-satisfaction and defiance, and his long struggle is here represented in a sympathetic light. This final reversal of the moral judgment is even more apparent in the magazine version of the novel, in which Fitzgerald not only defended the grandeur of Anthony's and Gloria's desperate attempt, but went so far as to exalt the validity of its motivation—"the freshness and fulness of their desire." "Their fault was not that they had doubted but that they had believed," Fitzgerald had written. Their only "disastrous extremes" were identified with "the exquisite perfection of their boredom, the delicacy of their inattention, the inexhaustibility of their discontent," and their figures acquired a halo of romantic suffering and purity. It is worthwhile quoting the whole final passage of the magazine version, which justifies, among other things, the title of the last chapter ("Together with the Sparrows") which was retained in the book:

That exquisite heavenly irony which had tabulated the demise of many generations of sparrows seems to us to be content with the moral judgments of man upon fellow man. If there is a subtle and yet more nebulous ethic somewhere in the mind, one might believe that beneath the sordid dress and near the bruised heart of this transaction there was a motive which was not weak but only futile and sad. In the search for happiness, which search is the greatest and possibly the only crime of which we in our petty misery are capable, these two people were marked as guilty chiefly by the freshness and fulness of their desire. Their illusion was always a comparative thing—they had sought glamor and color through their respective worlds with steadfast loyalty—sought it and it alone in kisses and in wine, sought it with the same ingenuousness in the wanton moonlight as under the cold sun of inviolate chastity. Their fault was not that they had doubted but that they had believed.

The exquisite perfection of their boredom, the delicacy of their inattention, the inexhaustibility of their discontent—were disastrous extremes—that was all. And if, before Gloria yielded up her gift of beauty, she shed one bright feather of light so that someone, gazing up from the grey earth, might say, "Look! There is an angel's wing!" perhaps she had given more than enough for her tinsel joys.[3]

[3] In *The Metropolitan Magazine,* LV (March 1922), p. 113; see also *Letters,* p. 152.

The logical development of the story is here given a deliberate twist; and it is perhaps significant that this idea of a moral comment on his characters that would justify their struggle and explain its motivations came to Fitzgerald, it seems, at the last moment and in a sudden flash, since in the manuscript version of the novel the story closed simply with the return of Gloria to her Paradise:

> The stars greeted her intimately as they went by and the winds made a soft welcoming flurry in the air. Sighing, she began a conversation with a voice that was in the white wind.
> "Back again," the voice whispered.
> "Yes."
> "After fifteen years."
> "Yes."
> The voice hesitated.
> "How remote you are," it said, "Unstirred. . . . You seem to have no heart. How about the little girl? The glory of her eyes is gone—"
> But Beauty had forgotten long ago.

Such a conclusion probably belonged to an early conception of the novel, when Gloria *(la belle dame sans merci)* was to be represented as the main cause of Anthony's deterioration and ruin. But it makes it clear that Fitzgerald had not completely mastered his material when he published the novel and that his final rehabilitation of Anthony was due to a sudden impulse which reflected, somehow, a basic uncertainty as to his real stature and accomplishments. Traces of this wavering attitude toward Anthony can in fact be found in other passages of the book as well, and they must be acknowledged, even if it means recognizing that *The Beautiful and Damned* does not present a story as straightforward as one would like to have it.

Consider, for instance, the nature of Anthony's relationship with his few friends, especially at the beginning. It is clear that he enjoys an unquestionable superiority over Maury Noble and Richard Caramel, but even after his "downfall" Fitzgerald represents him as superior to both Noble and Caramel. It is true that Noble, in spite of his nihilistic tirade in the middle of the book (at the end of the chapter entitled "Symposium"), succumbs to a respectable, middle-class marriage, and that Caramel undertakes a brilliant career as a commercial novelist—a career which gives him fame and fortune, but does not redeem him from the limitations of his talent and the meanness of his compromises. Still, Anthony does not do any better than they: but by using these two figures, Fitzgerald apparently wished to set off in relief the purity, "the exquisite perfection" and the inaccessibility of Anthony, who remains true to his initial ideals without ever descending to a vulgar compromise. This is made quite clear in an episode toward the end, when poor Caramel is violently abused by Anthony, and Fitzgerald seems to watch the performance with great gusto.

The same might be said, with different qualifications, of Gloria, whose fascinating personality predominates in many episodes of the book and whose charm is felt both by Fitzgerald and the reader. But even if Fitzgerald's intent—conscious or unconscious—was to extol the "beauty" of his two characters by contrasting them with the mediocrity of middle-class life and ideals, we must still say that the remedy proposed is worse than the evil indicated and that this alternative to reality denies its own reasons, because the two protagonists are "damned" without hope by their actions and attitudes, as they are developed and made apparent in the story. And they are damned not only in the eyes of the world, or for moralistic considerations on the part of the readers, but because their story *is* a story of self-destruction, which naturally results in inner and outer ruin.

All this must be taken into consideration to understand the exact nature and quality of the book and its deeper meaning, in spite of the many misleading suggestions that we have to confront. *The Beautiful and Damned* is not "a distressing tragedy which should be, also, one hundred percent meaningless," as Edmund Wilson claimed, if we see beyond the surface into its *objective* line of development. And it is not a mere "muddle" in the presentation of the two characters, as Arthur Mizener maintained,[4] if we see their true natures behind the screen of their self-complacency. The book has a meaning and a significance, even if its theme is not rigorously focused and consistently developed to its logical conclusion.

The reason for this incongruity lies perhaps in the fact that Fitzgerald's attempt was too ambitious. Soon after his autobiographical *This Side of Paradise,* he was facing a new and com-

---

[4] Cf. Mizener, *The Far Side of Paradise,* p. 140. Wilson's essay "S.F." had appeared in *The Bookman,* March 1922. See also William Troy, "Scott Fitzgerald—The Authority of Failure" (1945), and J. F. Powers, "Dealers in Diamonds and Rhinestones," both in A. Kazin (ed.) *F. Scott Fitzgerald.*

plex theme which required a considerable amount of objective
treatment. Amory had been a direct projection of the writer
himself. To Anthony and Gloria he gave many characteristics,
traits, and apprehensions of his own and of his wife, but he
imagined his characters' experience as a possibility, rather than
representing his own private experience. It was not simply a
question of evoking or recreating a personal reality—it was
rather a question of bringing to life an imaginary situation,
which he had contemplated as a possibility, with no immediate
connection with his own life, and which was to be represented
in its objective development.[5] In this ambitious attempt Fitzgerald
proved himself unequal to the exacting task of controlling the
objective development of his characters according to a rigorous
thematic principle. He tried to detach himself from his characters,
to stand aside and unfold their story in all its implications, going so
far as to pass a moral judgment on them. On the other hand, he
sympathized with his characters and shared some of their illusions
and not a few of their attitudes, with the result that he felt like
justifying, incongruously, the greatness of their attempt. He had, in
other words, to expose and denounce two characters who appealed
to him, or to justify their beauty in spite of their damnation. He
wanted to do both things, and the thematic unity of the book was
seriously compromised. The double choice offered in the title is
reflected in the lack of a consistent resolution of its conflicting
motives. The objective and inescapable result of the action is that
Anthony and Gloria are "damned": and they cannot be, therefore, as "beautiful" as the author tries to make them.

This is why we have to conclude that *The Beautiful and
Damned* is a transitional novel. It lies half-way between a youthful success and the achievement of maturity. But if it is a novel
of transition, it is so because some of the limitations of *This
Side of Paradise* were transcended. Flappers and philosophers
celebrate no triumphs in this novel. If they do seem to gain a
victory, it is soon shown to be illusory and deceptive, a subtle
form of irredeemable defeat, the snare of moral misery. Al-

[5] "Gloria [he wrote his daughter years later] was a more trivial and vulgar person than your mother. I can't really say there was any resemblance except in the
beauty and certain terms of expression she used, and also I naturally used many
circumstantial events of our early married life. However the emphases were entirely
different. We had a much better time than Anthony and Gloria did." As quoted in
The Far Side of Paradise, pp. 124–25. This did not prevent reviewers from inter-
preting the novel as autobiography.

though sympathizing with the defiant attitude of his heroes, Fitzgerald feels the need to pass a moral judgment on them, and even in their glamorous and careless way of life he reveals the hidden flaw of failure and defeat. In spite of his enthusiasms, in *The Beautiful and Damned* Fitzgerald is concerned with exposing the inner meaning of life, not with reproducing its brilliant surface alone; he is concerned with suffering and the bitter aspects of experience, not with its playful manifestations. "I guess I am too much of a moralist at heart"—he was to write in his notes—"and really want to preach at people in some acceptable form, rather than to entertain them."[6] This inclination— if not yet this intention—is already present in his second novel.

[6] *The Crack-Up,* p. 305 and *Letters,* p. 63; on the subject of Fitzgerald's moralism, cf. also *The Far Side of Paradise,* pp. 3–4, 16, and 18, among others.

Robert Ornstein

Scott Fitzgerald's Fable of East and West

He felt then that if the pilgrimage eastward of the rare poisonous flower of his race was the end of the adventure which had started westward three hundred years ago, if the long serpent of the curiosity had turned too sharp upon itself, cramping its bowels, bursting its shining skin, at least there had been a journey; like to the satisfaction of a man coming to die—one of those human things that one can never understand unless one has made such a journey and heard the man give thanks with the husbanded breath. The frontiers were gone—there were no more barbarians. The short gallop of the last great race, the polyglot, the hated and the despised, the crass and scorned, had gone—at least it was not a meaningless extinction up an alley. (*The Crack-Up,* p. 199)

After a brief revival, the novels of Scott Fitzgerald seem destined again for obscurity, labeled this time, by their most recent critics, as darkly pessimistic studies of America's spiritual and ideological failures. *The Great Gatsby,* we are now told, is not simply a chronicle of the Jazz Age but rather a dramatization of the betrayal of the naïve American dream in a corrupt society.[1] I would agree that in *Gatsby* Fitzgerald did create a myth with the imaginative sweep of America's historical adventure across

[1] See Edwin Fussell, "Fitzgerald's Brave New World," *ELH,* XIX (Dec. 1952), 291–306; Marius Bewley, "Scott Fitzgerald's Criticism of America," *SR,* LXII (Spring 1954), 223–246; John W. Bicknell, "The Waste Land of F. Scott Fitzgerald," *VQR,* XXX (Autumn 1954). A somewhat different but equally negative interpretation is R. W. Stallman's "Gatsby and the Hole in Time," *MFS,* I (Nov. 1955), 1–15.

From College English, *XVIII (December 1956), 139–143. Copyright* © *1956 by the National Council of Teachers of English. Reprinted by permission of the publisher and Robert Ornstein.*

an untamed continent. But his fable of East and West is little concerned with twentieth-century materialism and moral anarchy,
for its theme is the unending quest of the romantic dream, which
is forever betrayed in face and yet redeemed in men's minds.

From the start, Fitzgerald's personal dreams of romance contained the seeds of their own destruction. In his earliest works,
his optimistic sense of the value of experience is overshadowed by
a personal intuition of tragedy; his capacity for naïve wonder
is chastened by satiric and ironic insights which make surrender
to the romantic impulse incomplete. Though able to idealize the
sensuous excitement of an exclusive party or a lovely face, Fitzgerald could not ignore the speciosity inherent in the romantic
stimuli of his social world—in the unhurried gracious poise that
money can buy. Invariably he studied what fascinated him so
acutely that he could give at times a clinical report on the very
rich, whose world seemed to hold the promise of a life devoid of
the vulgar and commonplace. A literalist of his own imagination (and therefore incapable of self-deception), he peopled extravagant fantasy with superbly real "denizens of Broadway." The result in the earlier novels is not so much an uncertainty of tone as
a curious alternation of satiric and romantic moments—a breath-
less adoration of flapper heroines whose passionate kisses are
tinged with frigidity and whose daring freedom masks an adolescent desire for the reputation rather than the reality of experience.

The haunting tone of *Gatsby* is more than a skillful fusion of
Fitzgerald's satiric and romantic contrarieties. Nick Carraway,
simultaneously enchanted and repelled by the variety of life,
attains Fitzgerald's mature realization that the protective enchantment of the romantic ideal lies in its remoteness from actuality.
He knows the fascination of yellow windows high above the city
streets even as he looks down from Myrtle Wilson's gaudy, smoke-
filled apartment. He still remembers the initial wonder of Gatsby's
parties long after he is sickened by familiarity with Gatsby's uninvited guests. In one summer Nick discovers a profoundly melancholy esthetic truth: that romance belongs not to the present but
to a past transfigured by imagined memory and to the illusory
promise of an unrealizable future. Gatsby, less wise than Nick,
destroys himself in an attempt to seize the green light in his own
fingers.

At the same time that Fitzgerald perceived the melancholy
nature of romantic illusion, his attitude towards the very rich crys-
talized. In *Gatsby* we see that the charming irresponsibility of

the flapper has developed into the criminal amorality of Daisy Buchanan, and that the smug conceit of the Rich Boy has hardened into Tom Buchanan's arrogant cruelty. We know in retrospect that Anthony Patch's tragedy was not his "poverty," but his possession of the weakness and purposelessness of the very rich without their protective armor of wealth.

The thirst for money is a crucial motive in *Gatsby* as in Fitzgerald's other novels, and yet none of his major characters are materialists, for money is never their final goal. The rich are too accustomed to money to covet it. It is simply the badge of their "superiority" and the justification of their consuming snobberies. For those who are not very rich—for the Myrtle Wilsons as well as the Jay Gatsbys—it is the alchemic reagent that transmutes the ordinary worthlessness of life. Money is the demiurgos of Jimmy Gatz's Platonic universe, and the proof, in "Babylon Revisited," of the unreality of reality (". . .the snow of twenty-nine wasn't real snow. If you didn't want it to be snow, you just paid some money"). Even before *Gatsby,* in "The Rich Boy," Fitzgerald had defined the original sin of the very rich: They do not worship material gods but they "possess and enjoy early, and it does something to them, makes them soft where we are hard, and cynical where we are trustful. . . ." Surrounded from childhood by the artificial security of wealth, accustomed to owning rather than wanting, they lack anxiety or illusion, frustration or fulfillment. Their romantic dreams are rooted in the adolescence from which they never completely escape—in the excitement of the prom or petting party, the reputation of being fast on the college gridiron or the college weekend.

Inevitably, then, Fitzgerald saw his romantic dream threaded by a double irony. Those who possess the necessary means lack the will, motive, or capacity to pursue a dream. Those with the heightened sensitivity to the promises of life have it because they are the disinherited, forever barred from the white palace where "the king's daughter, the golden girl" awaits "safe and proud above the struggles of the poor." Amory Blaine loses his girl writing advertising copy at ninety a month. Anthony Patch loses his mind after an abortive attempt to recoup his fortune peddling bonds. Jay Gatsby loses his life even though he makes his millions because they are not the kind of safe, respectable money that echoes in Daisy's lovely voice. The successful entrepreneurs of Gatsby's age are the panderers to vulgar tastes, the high pressure salesmen, and, of course, the bootleggers. Yet once, Fitzgerald suggests, there had been opportunity commensurate with aspiration, an unexplored and unexploited frontier where great fortunes had been made or at least romantically stolen. And out of the shifting of opportunities from the West to Wall Street, he creates an American fable which redeems as well as explains romantic failure.

But how is one to accept, even in fable, a West characterized by the dull rectitude of Minnesota villages and an East epitomized by the sophisticated dissipation of Long Island society? The answer is perhaps that Fitzgerald's dichotomy of East and West has the poetic truth of James's antithesis of provincial American virtue and refined European sensibility. Like *The Portrait of a Lady* and *The Ambassadors, Gatsby* is a story of "displaced persons" who have journeyed eastward in search of a larger experience of life. To James this reverse migration from the New to the Old World has in itself no special significance. To Fitzgerald, however, the lure of the East represents a profound displacement of the American dream, a turning back upon itself of the historic pilgrimage towards the frontier which had, in fact, created and sustained that dream. In *Gatsby* the once limitless western horizon is circumscribed by the "bored, sprawling, swollen towns beyond the Ohio, with their interminable inquisitions which spared only the children and the very old." The virgin territories of the frontiersman have been appropriated by the immigrant families, the diligent Swedes — the unimaginative, impoverished German farmers like Henry Gatz. Thus after a restless nomadic existence, the Buchanans settle "permanently" on Long Island because Tom would be "a God damned fool to live anywhere else." Thus Nick comes to New York with a dozen volumes on finance which promise "to unfold the shining secrets that only Midas, Morgan and Maecenas knew." Gatsby's green light, of course, shines in only one direction—from the East across the continent to Minnesota, from the East across the bay to his imitation mansion in West Egg.

Lying in the moonlight on Gatsby's deserted beach, Nick realizes at the close just how lost a pilgrimage Gatsby's had been:

> . . . I became aware of the old island here that had flowered once for Dutch sailors' eyes—a fresh, green breast of the new world. Its vanished trees, the trees that had made way for Gatsby's house, had once pondered in whispers to the last and greatest of all human dreams; for a transitory moment man must have held his breath in the presence of this continent, compelled into an aesthetic contemplation he neither understood nor desired, face to face for the last time in history with something commensurate to his capacity for wonder.

Gatsby is the spiritual descendant of these Dutch sailors. Like them, he set out for gold and stumbled on a dream. But he journeys in the wrong direction in time as well as space. The transitory enchanted moment has come and gone for him and for the others, making the romantic promise of the future an illusory reflection of the past. Nick still carries with him a restlessness born of the war's excitement; Daisy silently mourns the romantic adventure of her "white" girlhood; Tom seeks the thrill of a vanished football game. Gatsby devotes his life to recapturing a love lost five years before. When the present offers nothing commensurate with man's capacity for wonder, the romantic credo is the belief—Gatsby's belief— in the ability to repeat the disembodied past. Each step towards the green light, however, shadows some part of Gatsby's grandiose achievement. With Daisy's disapproval the spectroscopic parties cease. To preserve her reputation Gatsby empties his mansion of lights and servants. And finally only darkness and ghostly memories tenant the deserted house as Gatsby relives his romantic past for Nick after the accident.

Like his romantic dream Jay Gatsby belongs to a vanished past. His career began when he met Dan Cody, a debauched relic of an earlier America who made his millions in the copper strikes. From Cody he received an education in ruthlessness which he applied when the accident of the war brought him to the beautiful house of Daisy Fay. In the tradition of Cody's frontier, he "took what he could get, ravenously and unscrupulously," but in taking Daisy he fell in love with her. "She vanished into her rich house, into her rich full life, leaving Gatsby—nothing. He felt married to her, that was all."

"He felt married to her"—here is the reaction of bourgeois conscience, not of calculating ambition. But then Gatsby is not really Cody's protégé. Jimmy Gatz inherited an attenuated version of the American dream of success, a more moral and genteel dream suited to a nation arriving at the respectability of established wealth and class. Respectability demands that avarice be masked with virtue, that personal aggrandizement pose as self-improvement. Success is no longer to the cutthroat or the ruthless but to the diligent and the industrious, to the boy who scribbles naïve resolves on the flyleaf of *Hopalong Cassidy*. Fabricated of pulp fiction clichés (the impoverished materials of an extraordinary imagination), Gatsby's dream of self-improvement blossoms into a preposterous tale of ancestral wealth and culture. And his dream is incorruptible because his great enterprise is not side-street "drugstores," or stolen bonds, but himself, his fictional past, his mansion, and his gaudy entertainments. Through it all he moves alone and untouched; he is the impresario, the creator, not the enjoyer of a riotous venture dedicated to an impossible goal.

It may seem ironic that Gatsby's dream of self-improvement is realized through partnership with Meyer Wolfsheim, but Wolfsheim is merely the post-war successor to Dan Cody and to the ruthlessness and greed that once exploited a virgin West. He is the fabulous manipulator of bootleg gin rather than of copper, the modern man of legendary accomplishment "who fixed the World's Series back in 1919." The racketeer, Fitzgerald suggests, is the last great folk hero, the Paul Bunyan of an age in which romantic wonder surrounds underworld "gonnegtions" instead of raw courage or physical strength. And actually Gatsby is destroyed not by Wolfsheim, or association with him, but by the provincial squeamishness which makes all the Westerners in the novel unadaptable to life in the East.

Despite her facile cynicism and claim to sophistication, Daisy is still the "nice" girl who grew up in Louisville in a beautiful house with a wicker settee on the porch. She remains "spotless," still immaculately dressed in white and capable of a hundred whimsical, vaporous enthusiasms. She has assimilated the urbane ethic of the East which allows a bored wife a casual discreet affair. But she cannot, like Gatsby's uninvited guests, wink at the illegal and the criminal. When Tom begins to unfold the sordid details of Gatsby's career, she shrinks away; she never intended to leave her husband, but now even an affair is impossible. Tom's provinciality is more boorish than genteel. He has assumed the role of Long Island country gentleman who keeps a mistress in a midtown apartment. But with Myrtle Wilson by his side he turns the role into a ludicrous travesty. By nature a libertine, by upbringing a prig, Tom shatters Gatsby's facade in order to preserve his "gentleman's" conception of womanly virtue and of the sanctity of his marriage.

Ultimately, however, Gatsby is the victim of his own smalltown notions of virtue and chivalry. "He would never so much as look at a friend's wife"—or at least he would never try to steal her in her husband's house. He wants Daisy to say that she never loved Tom because only in this way can the sacrament of Gatsby's "marriage" to her in Louisville—his prior claim—be recognized. Not content merely to repeat the past, he must also eradicate the years in which his dream lost its reality. But the dream, like the vanished frontier which it almost comes to represent, is lost forever "somewhere back in that vast obscurity beyond the city, where the dark field of the republic rolled on under the night."

After Gatsby's death Nick prepares to return to his Minnesota home, a place of warmth and enduring stability, carrying with him a surrealistic night vision of the debauchery of the East. Yet his return is not a positive rediscovery of the wellsprings of American life. Instead it seems a melancholy retreat from the ruined promise of the East, from the empty present to the childhood memory of the past. Indeed, it is this childhood memory, not the reality of the West which Nick cherishes. For he still thinks the East, despite its nightmarish aspect, superior to the stultifying small-town dullness from which he fled. And by the close of *Gatsby* it is unmistakably clear that the East does not symbolize contemporary decadence and the West the pristine virtues of an earlier America. Fitzgerald does not contrast Gatsby's criminality with his father's unspoiled rustic strength and dignity. He contrasts rather Henry Gatz's dull, gray, almost insentient existence, "a meaningless extinction up an alley," with Gatsby's pilgrimage Eastward, which, though hopeless and corrupting, was at least a journey of life and hope—an escape from the "vast obscurity" of the West that once spawned and then swallowed the American dream. Into this vast obscurity the Buchanans finally disappear. They are not Westerners any longer, or Easterners, but merely two of the very rich, who in the end represent nothing but themselves. They are careless people. Tom and Daisy, selfish, destructive, capable of anything except human sympathy, and yet not sophisticated enough to be really decadent. Their irresponsibility, Nick realizes, is that of pampered children, who smash up "things and creatures . . . and let other people clean up the mess." They live in the eternal moral adolescence which only wealth can produce and protect.

By ignoring its context one can perhaps make much of Nick's indictment of the Buchanans. One can even say that in *The Great Gatsby* Fitzgerald adumbrated the coming tragedy of a nation grown decadent without achieving maturity—a nation that possessed and enjoyed early and in its arrogant assumption of superiority lost sight of the dream that had created it. But is it not absurd to interpret Gatsby as a mythic Spenglerian anti-hero? Gatsby *is* great, because his dream, however naïve, gaudy, and unattainable is one of the grand illusions of the race, which keep men from becoming too old or too wise or too cynical of their human limitations. Scott Fitzgerald's fable of East and West does not lament the decline of American civilization. It mourns the eternal lateness of the present hour suspended between the past of romantic memory and the future of romantic promise which ever recedes before us.

John W. Bicknell

The Waste Land of F. Scott Fitzgerald

At this late date it may seem superfluous to say anything more about Fitzgerald: the roses have been strewn, the critics have been collected by Alfred Kazin, and the pro's and con's laid end to end. Yet I feel that another word must be said, for the revival of interest in Fitzgerald is a cultural phenomenon worth our curiosity. One point may be made immediately: we have stopped talking as if Fitzgerald's importance consisted in being a charming echo of the Jazz Age. We are beginning to see that his evocation of that age carries with it ominous tones of impending disaster. Fitzgerald could hardly complain now as he did to Edmund Wilson that not one of the reviewers of *Gatsby* "had the slightest idea what the book was about."

In 1925 it was perhaps difficult to take seriously a writer who portrayed the beautiful and the rich as essentially damned and who implied that the American Dream was, after all, little more than a thinly veiled nightmare. In the 1950s we are less likely to misunderstand his intentions. Increasingly, modern critics are recognizing that *The Great Gatsby* is a searching critique of American society. In fact, some of our pundits are elevating Fitzgerald into the first order of American writers almost entirely on the strength of his gloomy cadences. Those who take Fitzgerald closest to their bosoms seem to be the ones who are always lecturing us on the necessity of having a tragic sense of life. But is the tendency of Fitzgerald's art essentially tragic, or is it merely pessimistic?

As we reread *Gatsby* today, we are struck by the sharpness

Reprinted from the Virginia Quarterly Review, *XXX (Autumn 1954), 556–572, by permission of the author and publisher.*

with which he seized upon the archetypal theme of the twenties and thirties, and by the fact that he pronounced a sentence of doom over a social order that imagined itself in full flower. For indeed, the atmosphere, the characterizations, and the final violence of *Gatsby* all resound with the chords of moral horror and disillusion. It is, as Lionel Trilling has hinted, a prose version of Eliot's "Waste Land," a poem Fitzgerald knew almost by heart. The prevailing tone is brooding, haunted, elegiac.

Central to the novel's total effect, as in Eliot's poem, are symbols and images of waste, desolation, and futility. From the outset, the landscape is charged with symbolic overtones. Chapter II begins with a description, Eliot-like in tone and implication, Conrad-like in cadence:

> About halfway between West Egg and New York the motor road hastily joins the railroad and runs beside it for a quarter of a mile, so as to shrink away from a certain desolate area of land. This is the valley of ashes—a fantastic farm where ashes grow like wheat into ridges and hills and grotesque gardens; where ashes take the forms of houses and chimneys and rising smoke and, finally, with a transcendent effort, of ash-gray men who move dimly and are already crumbling through the powdery air. . . .

This is the Valley of Dry Bones, the Waste Land, the dusty replica of modern society, where ash-gray men are crumbling, like Eliot's hollow men. The camera focuses next on the monstrous image of an oculist's billboard—the blue and gigantic eyes of Doctor T. J. Eckleburg, which "look out of no face," but from "a pair of enormous yellow spectacles," and "dimmed a little by many paintless days over sun and rain, brood on over the solemn dumping ground." This grotesque image, reappearing throughout the story, eventually becomes a symbol of what God has become in the modern world, an all-seeing deity—indifferent, faceless, blank. Reading these pages instantly reminds one of Eliot's lines:

> What are the roots that clutch, what branches grow
> Out of this stony rubbish? Son of man,
> You cannot say, or guess, for you know only
> A heap of broken images, where the sun beats
> And the dead tree gives no shelter. . . .

Fitzgerald augments this sense of hopelessness by descriptions of New York in the dense summer heat. Occasionally he gives us pathetic images of sterility reminiscent of Eliot's "Preludes" or of the "Unreal City" passages in "The Waste Land." Seeing these images, Nick Carraway, the narrator, soon loses his fondness for New York:

> At the enchanted metropolitan twilight I felt a haunting loneliness sometimes, and felt it in others—poor young clerks who loitered in front of windows waiting until it was time for a solitary restaurant dinner—young clerks in the dusk, wasting the most poignant moments of night and life.

More effective, perhaps because less self-consciously underlined, are such scenes as the party in Myrtle Wilson's apartment, an image of an action symbolizing hollow lives and empty relationships. In this sordid orgy, the sham camaraderie of whiskey only emphasizes the absence of any really human or humane contacts. In fact, everything that takes place in the city gives the lie to Jordan Baker's easy assertion that "there's something sensuous about [New York]—overripe, as if all sorts of funny fruits were going to fall into your hands."

Moreover, a moment's glance at Fitzgerald's characters reminds us that in his vision of society we have only a choice of mindless evils or pathetic follies. Tom Buchanan, the wealthy ex-athlete from Yale, is a liar, a hypocrite, and a bully. The splendor of his surroundings is equaled only by his stupidity and "hard malice." Today we would call him the perfect example of the upper-class Fascist, who, obsessed with fear that the black races may overthrow "Nordic Supremacy," sees himself "on the last barrier of civilization." His fear, however, sharpens his cunning, and his position in society gives him the opportunity to use it. Not only does he lie to Myrtle Wilson, but with ruthless contempt, he exploits her husband, George, as an instrument of revenge on Gatsby. Morally speaking, he is Gatsby's murderer.

Tom's wife, Daisy, suggests the callous *ennui* of the beautiful society matron. She is ready to play with Gatsby, partially out of nostalgia for their youthful romance, partially to spite the philandering Tom, but more, one feels, as a relief from boredom. "What do people plan?" she asks, and the sentence is symbolic of her emptiness; she is like Eliot's lady in "The Waste Land" who cries out, "What shall we do tomorrow? What shall we ever do?" Ironically enough, it is Gatsby who finally isolates the quality of her voice. "Her voice is full of money," he suddenly remarks; she is the "king's daughter . . . the golden girl." The suspenseful play of irony around the ambiguous connotations of "golden" finally resolves when we discover that the golden girl is really made of bronze. If she does not love Tom, she shares his callous selfishness. With him she conspires to sacrifice Jay Gatsby to her own safety, and is in a real sense an accomplice in the final crime.

The victims—Myrtle and George Wilson, and Jay Gatsby— are not so much vicious as pathetic. Members of the lower middle class, the Wilsons are led to ruin by following ill-conceived dreams of escaping from their dreary lives into the world of glamour. Myrtle, who in her energy resembles Gatsby, seeks escape in an affair with Tom Buchanan. To be "ladylike" she buys a dog; in tawdry finery she queens it over the guests in "her" apartment; but when she tries to assert herself, Tom breaks her nose. Myrtle's last desperate effort to escape ends in violent death, thus mercifully sparing her the knowledge that she was merely Tom's plaything.

Her husband, George, is even more pathetic. He is a sick man, too weak to summon up the energy to provide his life either with significance or with the means of escape. Only in the hysteria incited by the betrayal of his home and the death of his wife does he achieve a moment of intense experience, and what is born in hysteria dies in futile violence. Like many in his position, George is conscious of hostility and frustration, but unaware of the forces pressing on him. Under these circumstances his rebellion proves to be misdirected and self-destructive. Deluded by his obeisance to the rich, George seeks help from Tom Buchanan, his betrayer both in love and in revenge. It is an all too familiar pattern: the rich and powerful maintaining their status by directing middle-class frustrations into fratricidal struggles against scapegoats.

Most poignant, however, is the figure of Jay Gatsby. Coming from the Middle West, where the Horatio Alger traditions of self-reliance and enterprise still had some vitality, he is a Clyde Griffiths with energy and know-how. Though he has more control over his destiny than Dreiser's hapless young man, Jay, like Clyde, is destroyed by uncritically following his fantasies. Gatsby has dreamed of riches as a means of achieving the golden vision of love and life with his old sweetheart, Daisy. To make this dream come true, he has built a fortune on fraud and violence. He is, as Charles Weir reminds us, the perverted version of the self-made man, Horatio Alger turned bootlegger and mobster, but whose dream of success and the golden girl, Fitzgerald tries to assure us, is still unsullied. In the eyes of Carraway, Jay's "sensitivity to the promises of life," and his capacity for hope and innocent wonder make him a moral angel compared to the Buchanans, the respectable corrupters of the American Dream.

The intensity of Gatsby's dream has, in fact, made him childishly naïve. He is blithely confident that he can regain Daisy and their youthful ecstasy merely by displaying to her his ability for conspicuous waste. To Carraway's warning that "You can't repeat the past," he answers, "Why of course you can." So real has his sentimental vision of Daisy become that he refuses to believe that she has ever cared for Tom, and when in the Plaza suite Tom exposes him for what he is, Jay is unable to detect the revulsion on Daisy's face. The illusion persists. After the accident which kills Myrtle, he chivalrously plans to shoulder the blame for Daisy's careless driving. After taking her home, he stands outside her window deluded in the belief that she needs protection from Tom, totally unaware that she is busily planning with Tom ways and means for escaping the consequences. Gatsby, a man capable of organizing a bootlegger's ring, is here as helpless as a child. Like George Wilson who kills him, Gatsby dies ignorant of the forces that preyed upon him and of the essentially infantile quality of his dreams. His death is pathetic rather than tragic; he is a victim, not a hero.

Thus, the novel ends, as it began, in pessimism, a pessimism induced by Fitzgerald's recognition of the forces that "preyed on Gatsby" and "the foul dust that floated in the wake of his dream." Carraway leaves New York haunted by meaningless violence and futile lies; nothing and no one in America gives him hope. He speaks of the "bored, sprawling, swollen towns beyond the Ohio, with their interminable inquisitions which spared only the children and the very old," while the East haunts him "like a night scene from El Greco." In the foreground he sees an Eliot-like image, symbolic of futility:

> Four solemn men in dress suits are walking along the sidewalk with a stretcher on which lies a drunken woman in a white evening dress. Her arm, which dangles over the side, sparkles cold with jewels. Gravely the men turn in at a house—the wrong house. But no one knows the woman's name, and no one cares.

From this vision of useless damnation, his thought moves into an elegy for the lost wonder of America and the defeated wonder of

Gatsby, the latter felt as a sorry fragment of the former music; he has died like Sweeney among the nightingales of the Sacred Heart. Carraway's nostalgia for "the old island here that flowered once for Dutch sailors' eyes," and which "had once pandered in whispers to the last and greatest of all human dreams," is unrelieved by hope for the future. Gatsby ends with a bang, and Carraway with a whimper; in that mournful conclusion, deep in *lacrimae rerum,* there are no fragments to shore against the ruins.

The parallel to Eliot suggests another—that of Conrad. In fact, as the dependence of Eliot's "The Hollow Men" on "The Heart of Darkness" makes obvious, the influence is interrelated. Like Conrad, Fitzgerald was fascinated by the man with the romantic dream who is nonetheless a moral failure. Gatsby is in some ways akin to Lord Jim and to Kurtz. On the surface he is like the "excessively romantic" Jim; "there was," Fitzgerald tells us, "something gorgeous about him, some heightened sensibility to the promises of life . . . a gift for hope, a romantic readiness. . . ." But the parallel with Kurtz is closer. Gatsby, like Kurtz, blends a romantic vision with bloody and violent means, but unlike Kurtz, never comprehends himself or understands his own contradictions. Yet the most significant analogy lies in the cognate positions of Carraway and Marlow; they both face the same kind of choice. Just as Marlow identifies himself with Kurtz rather than with the mindless viciousness of the manager's crowd, so Carraway prefers Gatsby, the bootlegger with a dream, to the hard malice of the Buchanans. ("They're a rotten crowd," he tells Gatsby. "You're worth the whole damn bunch put together.") The pessimism of both writers, implicit in the choice-between-evils theme, is accentuated by the fact that both, like Eliot, set the choice against a quasi-nostalgic vision of a past in which the romantic dream was presumably unsullied by foul dust. The fact that both see modern corruption in contrast to a lost rather than to an emergent ideal tends to make their art, like Eliot's, essentially elegiac. Conrad and Fitzgerald hold in common a hatred of unprincipled malice and dishonorable conduct; in neither is there any glimpse of new roads to honor. Writing before the first World War, Conrad was able to assume the posture of stoicism, a fact which saves his nostalgia from mawkishness or enervation; Fitzgerald, in 1925, is not entirely free of either. His final image is of passive capitulation: "So we beat on, boats against the current, borne back ceaselessly into the past."

Here then is Fitzgerald's waste land, the "spoiled priest's" brooding lament over the destruction of the American dream, a lament without a benediction and without even a hint of any means by which the waste land may be watered. In this sense, his portrait of modern American society was even more pessimistic than Eliot's, for at this stage and in this novel he seems to have been unable to adopt any attitude that might provide a means either for redeeming the time or enduring it. For him all gods were fallen so that Eliot's reactionary and ritualist solution was unacceptable. Like many of his generation, he was alienated "from the prevailing order"; like his own Amory Blaine, he even talked vaguely of socialism, but as he tells us in "Echoes of the Jazz Age," the alienation was "cynical rather than revolutionary." He could not believe in any crusade. Cut off, as Henry Dan Piper suggests, from "the imaginative resources of the liberal tradition, especially those of American literature," and isolated from the contemporary radical and liberal movements (themselves weak) which might have provided a taproot to hope, it is little wonder that Fitzgerald was incapable of being either a revolutionary, or a consolatory, or a tragic artist.

Though in 1933 he was to read Marx and later to declare himself "essentially a Marxian," and in 1940 even to advise his daughter to read Marx's chapter on "The Working Day," the overall evidence from his life and art indicates that what he shared with Marxism and liberalism was the awareness of social disease, not their prescriptions for its cure. In this sense he reminds us of Henry Adams, who watched with fear and horror the destruction of the old America by the robber barons, and who tried in vain to make himself a socialist. Both ended, like so many disaffected but essentially uncommitted liberals, in skepticism, in elegy, and in a feeling of tired emptiness.

A careful reading of Fitzgerald's later novels will not substantially change these conclusions. A development of a kind takes place, of course, but within the framework I have defined above, not as a break from it. *Tender Is the Night,* while its portrait of society's disintegration is more explicitly Marxist, is even more pessimistic than *Gatsby.* Dick Diver is repeatedly described as a victim of a private dream of money which makes his integrity vulnerable to the appeal of great wealth:

Watching his father's struggles in poor parishes had wedded a desire for money to an essentially unacquisitive nature. It was not a healthy necessity for security—he had never felt more sure of himself, more thoroughly his own man, than at the time of his marriage to Nicole. Yet he had been swallowed up like a gigolo, and somehow permitted his arsenal to be locked up in the Warren safety-deposit vaults.

Though this comes after the announcement of Abe North's violent death, we have been prepared for it by a description of Nicole, which might be called a capsule version of "Das Kapital":

> Nicole was the product of much ingenuity and toil. For her sake trains began their run in Chicago and traversed the round belly of the continent to California; chicle factories fumed and link belts grew link by link in factories; men mixed toothpaste in vats and drew mouthwash out of copper hogsheads; girls canned tomatoes quickly in August or worked rudely at the Five-and-Tens on Christmas Eve; half-breed Indians toiled on Brazilian coffee plantations and dreamers were muscled out of patent rights in new tractors—these were some of the people who gave a tithe to Nicole, and as the whole system swayed and thundered onward it lent a feverish bloom to such processes of hers as wholesale buying, like the flush of a fireman's face holding his post before a spreading blaze. She illustrated very simple principles, containing in herself her own doom. . . .

Though the kinship with Marx is obvious, one suspects that the cadence of the lines beginning "For her sake" and the structure of the whole passage owe a good deal to stanzas xiv–xv of Keats's "Isabella," of which Fitzgerald was so fond, and which Bernard Shaw asserted contained the essence of the "immense indictment of the profiteers and exploiters with which Marx had shaken capitalistic civilization to its foundations." Of course, neither Keats nor Fitzgerald shook any foundations. Fitzgerald, unlike Keats, even admires the grace with which Nicole illustrates the "feverish bloom" of decay. Nevertheless, the passage prepares the reader for the perception that Dr. Diver, the disintegrating paragon of grace, will give more than "a tithe to Nicole," and will become one with the girls canning tomatoes and the half-breed Indians on coffee plantations. He permits himself to be squeezed dry, and returns to America, ultimately to fade away into the obscurities of Hornell, New York. Here, too, as in *Gatsby,* our final image is of defeat.

The pessimism of this conclusion becomes all the more striking when we recall that Fitzgerald in his early plans for the novel went so far as to contemplate giving Dick Diver a son, who was to be sent to the Soviet Union. The son was to be a symbol of hope balancing the deterioration of the father. Fitzgerald rejected the scheme, and wisely too, for it is hard not to believe that however he handled the planned episode, it would have been a failure artistically. It would have been basically false, a hollow gesture, since it would not have represented any genuine feeling on Fitzgerald's part. The point is not that he was unable to believe in the Soviet Union as a symbol of hope, but rather that he could not find any images of hope or vitality either at home, or abroad, or within himself. The kind of belief in humanity that Steinbeck evoked dramatically in *The Grapes of Wrath* five years later was beyond Fitzgerald's sensibility and experience.

It is this fact that makes Fitzgerald open to the commonly-made charge that his heroes have insufficient stature. In 1934 William Troy complained that it was inaccurate to call *Tender Is the Night* a study in degeneration, "for such degeneration presupposes an anterior dignity or perfection of character." My own approach to this issue is from a different angle. I am less insistent than Troy that we see the tragic hero at a high point of "anterior dignity" from which he is cast down: we do not need paragons to have tragic heroes. What we do need is a man who, though no paragon, nevertheless conducts a struggle against the forces, both external and internal, which are destroying him. And this is the difficulty we meet in trying to extend our sympathies to Dick Diver. He goes down to defeat without struggling against his inner weakness or against the forces that have capitalized on it. Although Dick Diver recognizes what has happened to him, as Gatsby does not, his surrender makes him no less a victim. *L'homme épuisé* may well be one we can pity, or one through which we can see predatory forces at work, but his unwillingness to resist them, whatever his anterior dignity, robs him of heroic stature. Charles Weir writes that Fitzgerald's main theme is "the futility of effort and the necessity of struggle" and goes on to point out that Fitzgerald was never able to make this theme a noble one because he could not deal with the problem in his own life. We may well agree. We must add the essential point, however, by arguing from the novels as well as from biography, that Fitzgerald's failure to give his theme nobility lies in his inability to image forth the necessity of struggle.

Between *Tender Is the Night* and *The Last Tycoon,* Fitzgerald underwent the breakdown he records in *The Crack-up.* Here the waste land of the outer world was mirrored in the individual soul.

Both the wastefulness of his own life and of his era led him to the generalization that "all life is a process of breaking down." He realized that he had done very little thinking; and we may note that for all his ideal of the Goethe-Byron-Shaw "entire man," he had permitted his friends to take care of his ideas of the good life, his artistic conscience, and his personal relations. Even his political conscience, he admits, "had scarcely existed for ten years save as an element of irony." He also saw that he had become too much identified with "the objects of [his] horror or compassion," an identification which, he rightly says, "spells the death of accomplishment." He felt the need of making "a clean break" —not an escape, which he calls "an excursion into a trap," but "something you cannot come back from," a decision to "slay the empty shell who had been posturing at it for years."

But of what did Fitzgerald's complete break consist? As he tells us, he decided to be a writer only, to give up the ideal of the entire man, to cease to be a person, to cease "to be kind, just or generous." "There was to be no more giving of myself." He will let the "good people function as such," but for himself he will hang the sign *Cave Canem* over his door, though he realizes he will have to pay a price for this attitude. "How well," Weir asks, "did such bitterness serve him?" It is a good question and leads to others. To what extent did Fitzgerald really believe this decision constituted a clean break? To what degree does the decision to be "a writer only" detach one from the habit of "identification with the objects of one's horror or compassion"? To what extent does a "laughing stoicism" provide a basis for the ability to realize in literary terms "the necessity for struggle"? My answer would be that in Fitzgerald's case, his decision provided a basis only for enduring the time, but not for redeeming it; it gave him, perhaps, a cooler perspective on the social process which was his subject, but only partially, I believe, "that unshakable moral attitude towards the world we live in" that Dos Passos gives him credit for. He had begun with Marx and ended with Spengler. A clean break, a decision not to go home again, it seems to me, would have implied committing himself to struggle, and I see very little evidence of this either in *The Crack-up* or in *The Last Tycoon*.

Since *The Last Tycoon* is a fragment, generalizations must be tentative. However, from what remains we get a rather clear indication that Fitzgerald simultaneously returned to the objectivity he had displayed in *Gatsby* and advanced to a wider and more detailed presentation of his vision of the modern world.

Significantly, he carried his theme over from the *milieu* of smart-set *rentiers* into the world of industrial production. Whereas in *Gatsby* we are only dimly aware of Gatsby the organizer and man of action, in *The Last Tycoon,* we are made immediately aware of Monroe Stahr as a commanding personality at work at his job in the movie industry and in contact with its organized producers, its financial capital in New York, and its employees. For the first time in any of his major works Fitzgerald makes us directly conscious of a class struggle, not as in *Tender Is the Night,* where the workers are passive suppliers of leisure-class luxury, but in active terms with the employees as an organized force.

What we can see of *The Last Tycoon* is thus a realistic portrait of Hollywood and a cauterizing study of the deterioration of what Arthur Mizener calls the brilliant individual "who controlled everything with understanding and intelligence." Stahr is a Dick Diver in a position of power, a synthesis of Gatsby and Diver. It is, of course, the story of Stahr's defeat. Fitzgerald asserted that "it is not the story of deterioration—it is not depressing and not morbid in spite of the tragic ending."

Again, however, we must wonder if it was as tragic as he had hoped. From the beginning we see Stahr in a state of decay. We learn early that his heart is weak, his psyche split, and, as Fitzgerald portrays them, Stahr's directing and organizing activities are compulsive rather than controlled and purposeful. Equally compulsive is his love affair with Kathleen, an attempt like Gatsby's to recapture a past fragrance. He is eventually destroyed by inner contradictions exacerbated by the conflicts both within the industry and between the producers and the organized employees. As in his other novels Fitzgerald is recording and examining the death of a set of values, in short, of traditional individualism defeated in part by its own contradictions and in part by a plutocracy which has lost or never known the humanistic values once associated with individualism. This seems so obvious that it is puzzling to find one British critic writing that "at moments Stahr seems about to turn into that hero of our time, the man who is very rich and very 'Left'"; or to read William Troy's remark about Stahr's "last febrile gesture . . . his championship of the Hollywood underdog in a struggle with the racketeers and big producers."

It is important to establish the incorrectness of these readings of the novel, for otherwise we get the impression that at the end Fitzgerald made a leap to the left and created Stahr as some sort of "fellow traveler." This is pure nonsense. More illuminating is Mizener's statement that "Stahr was to be defeated primarily by the fact that in the modern kind of capitalist enterprise . . . there was no function for the brilliant individual who controlled everything by intelligence and understanding. . . . Yet, though Fitzgerald clearly felt this kind of man was doomed, and even rightly doomed, he admired his gifts. . . ." Moreover, for all Stahr's paternalistic interest in his employees, he is "driven by the logic of the situation," as Edmund Wilson puts it, "to fall in with" Brady's "idea of setting up a company union." This Stahr does after a vain effort to ease the 50 per cent wage cut ordered by Brady. In other words, when the lines were drawn, Stahr's hostility to unions pushes him into Brady's camp. This is hardly the portrait of a man who has gone "left"; Stahr is not the champion of the underdog, but of his own tattered ego and the remnants of his own integrity. Yet the loyalties that lead him to join forces with Brady more than threaten to destroy even what ego and integrity he may have left. As far as we can judge, Stahr was to have been shown eventually losing his position in the studio and getting himself embroiled in the struggle for power within the industry. This in turn was to lead him to adopt methods of blackmail and gangsterism and finally to plan the murder of Brady. Unlike Dick Diver, Stahr fights, but not for any positive value. Too late, he was to decide to call off the murder, but crash to death in a plane before carrying out the decision. This is the pattern of action which Fitzgerald's outline clearly lays down.

It is difficult to say whether *The Last Tycoon* would have become a tragedy. The ingredients are there: the man with large views, something of an artist, destroyed by an unilluminated individualism which lands him, despite his hatred of them, in the hands of his enemies. What remains in doubt is the way in which Fitzgerald would have handled Stahr's "recognition scene," when he decides to call off the murder of Brady. If his "recognition" was only to be the awareness that the decision to commit murder degraded him to the level of Brady, then he would have been only a slightly more self-conscious Gatsby, dying without real self-knowledge. If, on the other hand, he was to have realized that his basic flaw was his willingness to play into the hands of the men who are corrupting the whole film industry, then Stahr might well have emerged as a truly tragic hero. Had Fitzgerald succeeded in treating Stahr in this way, then one could accept Stephen Vincent Benét's assertion that Stahr "goes down whole"; as it is, we cannot tell, and therefore the statement is permanently premature.

There are hints that at the conclusion of the novel the emphasis was to be less on Stahr's self-realization, but more on the fact that with his death the movie industry is to be destroyed as a medium for artistry by the unscrupulous forces symbolized in the conscienceless company lawyer, Fleishacker. Stahr's funeral, Edmund Wilson tells us, was to have been "an orgy of Hollywood servility and hypocrisy." The negative emphasis of all this suggests that whereas Fitzgerald had achieved once more "the double vision" of Gatsby, he had still found no way out of his dilemma. The pattern of the novel reflects in art what he had set down as exposition in *The Crack-up,* where he imagines he is making a clean break from the state of mind that infected him. This view becomes the more credible when we notice that the images and symbols which he treats affirmatively and with affection are those that arouse a nostalgia for the past and indicate the distance of modern America from her past ideals. I am thinking particularly of the incident near the beginning where Cecilia, Willie White, and other movie professionals are held up by bad weather and try to find their way to Andrew Jackson's "Hermitage." As Edmund Wilson has suggested, the fact that they cannot get in is symbolic of the gap between the sordid present and a larger-visioned, more dignified democratic tradition. Though the elegiac note is suppressed, it is the only positive chord in the story as we have it.

It seems to me, then, that the burden of evidence suggests that *The Last Tycoon* would not have been the kind of tragedy in which the individuals die in full self-consciousness, so that the value they ultimately stand for, even though temporarily defeated, provides a meaning for their lives and for their deaths. Such a tragedy would have been a moving study of the impasse and defeat of a traditional individualism which finally grasps that its survival in a more meaningful form requires its reunion with a broader humanity, with Whitman's *en masse,* as well as a more than verbal recognition of the necessity of struggle. But Stahr's struggle takes place within the forces of decay, and his death was to be an accident.

If the logic of this study of Fitzgerald's Waste Land has any validity, then we must conclude that his literary achievement falls short of tragedy. For those of us concerned with the fate and problems of "The Liberal Imagination," a further conclusion suggests itself. In so far as insistence on the tragic sense of life urges us away from pollyanna optimism, the talk has been healthy. Too often, however, behind the call for a tragic sense of life lies, perhaps unconsciously, an identification of the tragic sense with the view that nothing can be done to alleviate modern man's physical and spiritual suffering. Sometimes I have felt that these critics have unwittingly become allied with Eliot's attack on liberalism and his defense of original (and therefore permanent) sin. All too frequently, the appeal to the tragic sense of life is made somehow to rationalize an apathy and a failure to try to discover, and act upon the discovery of, the forces in modern life which may well enable us to redeem the time as well as endure it, and of the springs of hope which can water the waste land and make the desert bloom. Whatever else tragedy may be, it is not apathy; it is not despair; it is not a form that induces the desire to capitulate to evil and suffering.

Alfred Kazin writes, "in a land of promise 'failure' will always be a classic theme." In this limited sense Fitzgerald's novels come within the purview of what may be defined as classic. His plot lines run on declining curves; nowhere are there lines of ascendance. He seems unable to give his reader images of integrative action or character, or of people or tendencies working in a positive direction. His world is in full Spenglerian decline. For the liberal and radical, a rereading of Fitzgerald's novels may well strengthen his conviction that contemporary society in its present stage is ruled by a complex of forces destructive of basic human values and subversive of man's vision of the good life. A greater number, however, receiving the same impression, may only be confirmed in their querulous apathy and provided with a further justification for self-pity, and for a passive, though disgruntled, acceptance of things as they are.

Kenneth E. Eble

The Craft of Revision: *The Great Gatsby*

"With the aid you've given me," Fitzgerald wrote Maxwell Perkins in December, 1924, "I can make *Gatsby* perfect."[1] Fitzgerald had sent the manuscript of the novel to Scribner's in late October, but the novel achieved its final form only after extensive revisions Fitzgerald made in the next four months. The pencil draft and the much revised galley proofs now in the Fitzgerald collection at Princeton library show how thoroughly and expertly Fitzgerald practiced the craft of revision.[2]

I

The pencil draft both reveals and masks Fitzgerald's struggles. The manuscript affords a complete first version, but the pages are not numbered serially from beginning to end, nor are the chapters and sections of chapters all tied together. There are three segments (one a copy of a previous draft) designated "Chapter III," two marked "Chapter VI." The amount of revising varies widely

[1] *The Letters of F. Scott Fitzgerald*, ed. Andrew Turnbull (New York, 1963), p. 172.

[2] This study is based on an examination of the original pencil draft and the galley proofs in the Fitzgerald collection in the Princeton Library and subsequent work with a microfilm copy of this material. I am indebted to the University of Utah Research Fund for a grant which enabled me to study the materials at Princeton, to Alexander P. Clark, curator of manuscripts, for his indispensable help in making this material available, and to Mr. Ivan Von Auw and the Fitzgerald estate for permission to use this material.

Reprinted from American Literature, *XXXVI (November 1964), 315–326, by permission of the publisher.*

from page to page and chapter to chapter; the beginning and end are comparatively clean, the middle most cluttered. Fitzgerald's clear, regular hand, however, imposes its own sense of order throughout the text. For all the revisions, the script goes about its business with a straightness of line, a regularity of letter that approaches formal elegance. When he is striking out for the first time, the writing tends to be large, seldom exceeding eight words per line or twenty-five lines per page. When he is copying or re-working from a previous draft, the writing becomes compressed — but never crabbed — and gets half again as much on a page.

An admirer of Fitzgerald — of good writing, for that matter — reads the draft with a constant sense of personal involvement, a sensation of small satisfied longings as the right word gets fixed in place, a feeling of strain when the draft version hasn't yet found its perfection of phrase, and a nagging sense throughout of how precariously the writer dangles between the almost and the attained. "All good writing," Fitzgerald wrote his daughter, "is *swimming under water* and holding your breath."[3]

At the beginning of the draft, there appears to have been little gasping for air. There at the outset, virtually as published, is that fine set piece which establishes the tone of the novel with the creation of Nick Carraway and his heightened sense of the fundamental decencies. As one reads the first chapter, however, the satisfaction of seeing the right beginning firmly established soon changes to surprise. The last page of the novel — "gradually I became aware of the old island here that flowered once for Dutch sailors' eyes — a fresh, green breast of the new world."[4] — was originally written as the conclusion of Chapter I. Some time before the draft went into the submission copy, Fitzgerald recognized that the passage was too good for a mere chapter ending, too definitive of the larger purposes of the book, to remain there. By the time the pencil draft was finished, that memorable paragraph had been put into its permanent place, had fixed the image of man holding his breath in the presence of the continent, "face to face for the last time in history with something commensurate to his capacity for wonder."

The three paragraphs which come immediately after, the last paragraphs of the novel, grew out of one long fluid sentence which was originally the final sentence of Chapter I in the draft: "And as

[3] *The Crack-Up,* p. 304.
[4] All citations hereafter are from the Scribner Library edition of *The Great Gatsby.*

I sat there brooding on the old unknown world I too held my breath and waited, until I could feel the motion of America as it turned through the hours—my own blue lawn and the tall incandescent city on the water and beyond that, the dark fields of the republic rolling on under the night." Fitzgerald expanded this suggestion into a full paragraph, crossed out the first attempt, and then rewrote it into three paragraphs on the final page of the draft. There, almost as it appears in the novel, is the green light on Daisy's dock ("green glimmer" in the draft), the orgiastic future (written "orgastic"),[5] and that ultimate sentence, "So we beat on, a boat [changed to "boats"] against the current, borne back ceaselessly into the past." So the draft ends, the last lines written in a "bold, swooping hand," as Fitzgerald described Gatsby's signature, a kind of autograph for the completed work.

The green light (there were originally two) came into the novel at the time of Daisy's meeting with Gatsby. "If it wasn't for the mist," he tells her, "we could see your house across the bay. You always have two green lights that burn all night at the end of your dock." Fitzgerald not only made the green light a central image of the final paragraph, but he went back to the end of the first chapter and added it there: "Involuntarily I glanced seaward —and distinguished nothing except a single green light, minute and far away, that might have been the end of a dock" (pp. 21–22).

II

Throughout the pencil draft, Fitzgerald made numerous revisions which bring out his chief traits as a reviser: he seldom threw anything good away, and he fussed endlessly at getting right things in the right places. The two parties at Gatsby's house, interesting as illustrations of Fitzgerald's mastery of the "scenic method," are equally interesting as examples of how he worked.

The purpose of the first party as it appears in the draft (Chapter III in the book) was chiefly that of creating the proper atmosphere. Though Gatsby makes his first appearance in this section,

---

[5] Arthur Mizener points out that Fitzgerald corrected the spelling from "orgastic" to "orgiastic" in his own copy of the book (*The Far Side of Paradise*, Boston, 1951, p. 336, n. 22). Yet Fitzgerald's letter to Maxwell Perkins, January 24, 1925, defends the original term: "'Orgastic' is the adjective for 'orgasm' and it expresses exactly the intended ecstasy. It's not a bit dirty" *(Letters,* p. 175*)*. The word appears as "orgiastic" in most editions of the novel, including the current Scribner's printings.

it is Gatsby's world that most glitters before our eyes. The eight servants (there were only seven in the draft), the five crates (only three in the draft) of oranges and lemons, the caterers spreading the canvas, the musicians gathering, the Rolls-Royce carrying party-goers from the city, are the kind of atmospherics Fitzgerald could always do well. The party itself as it unfolds in the draft reveals a number of intentions that Fitzgerald abandoned as he saw the possibilities of making the party vital to the grander design of the novel.

Originally, whether from strong feelings or in response to his readers' expectations, he took pains to bring out the wild and shocking lives being lived by many of Gatsby's guests. Drug addiction was apparently commonplace, and even more sinister vices were hinted at. A good deal of undergraduate party chatter was also cut from the draft. What a reader of the novel now remembers is what Fitzgerald brought into sharp relief by cutting out the distracting embellishments. "The Jazz History of the World" by Vladimir Tostoff (it was "Leo Epstien" [*sic*] originally; Fitzgerald deleted a number of "Jewish" remarks from the draft) was described in full. When Fitzgerald saw the galleys he called the whole episode "rotten" and reduced the page-and-a-half description to a single clause: "The nature of Mr. Tostoff's composition eluded me. . . ." (p. 50). By the time the party scene had been cut and reworked, almost all that remained was the introduction of Gatsby's physical presence into the novel and the splendid scene of Owl-Eyes in Gatsby's high Gothic library.

Among the many excisions in this party scene, one seemed far too good to throw away. In the draft, it began when Jordan Baker exchanges a barbed remark with another girl:

> "You've dyed your hair since then," remarked Miss Baker and I started but the girls had moved casually on and were talking to an elaborate orchid of a woman who sat in state under a white plum tree.
>
> "Do you see who that is?" demanded Jordan Baker interestly. [I use Fitzgerald's spelling here and elsewhere in quoting from the draft.]
>
> Suddenly I did see, with the peculiar unreal feeling which accompanies the recognition of a hitherto ghostly celebrity of the movies.
>
> "The man with her is her director," she continued. "He's just been married."
>
> "To her?"
>
> "No."

> She laughed. The director was bending over his pupil so eagerly that his chin and her mettalic black hair were almost in juxtaposition.
>
> "I hope he doesn't slip," she added. "And spoil her hair."
>
> It was still twilight but there was already a moon, produced no doubt like the turkey and the salad out of a caterer's basket. With her hard, slender golden arm drawn through mine we decended the steps. . . .

It is a fine scene, and the girl with the dyed hair, the moon, and the caterer's basket can be found on page 43 of the novel, so smoothly joined together that no one could suspect, much less mourn, the disappearance of that "elaborate orchid" of a woman. But, of course, she did not disappear. The scene was merely transported to the second party where the actress defined the second party as Owl-Eyes defined the first:

> "Perhaps you know that lady," Gatsby indicated a gorgeous, scarely human orchid of a woman who sat in state under a white-plum tree. Tom and Daisy stared, with the particularly unreal feeling that accompanies the recognition of a hitherto ghostly celebrity of the movies.
>
> "She's lovely," said Daisy.
>
> "The man bending over her is her director." (p. 106)

Two pages later, at the end of the second party, we see her again:

> It was like that. Almost the last thing I remember was standing with Daisy and watching the moving-picture director and his Star. They were still under the white-plum tree and their faces were touching except for a pale, thin ray of moonlight between. It occurred to me that he had been very slowly bending toward her all evening to attain this proximity, and even while I watched I saw him stoop one ultimate degree and kiss at her cheek.
>
> "I like her," said Daisy. "I think she's lovely."
>
> But the rest offended her. . . . (p. 108)

One can almost see the writer's mind in action here. The scene was first created, almost certainly, from the rightness of having a "ghostly celebrity of the movies" at the party. It first served merely as scenery and as a way of hinting at the moral laxity of Gatsby's guests. The need to compress and focus probably brought Fitzgerald to consider cutting it out entirely though it was obviously too good to throw away. By that time, perhaps, the second party scene had been written, another possibility had been opened up. Maybe at once, maybe slowly, Fitzgerald recognized that the scene could be used to capture Daisy's essential aloofness which was to defy even Gatsby's ardor. It may well be that this developed and practiced ability to use everything for its maximum effect, to strike no note, so to speak, without anticipating all its vibrations, is what separates Fitzgerald's work in *The Great Gatsby* from his earlier writing, what makes it seem such a leap from his first novels.

Among the many lessons Fitzgerald applied between the rough draft and the finished novel was that of cutting and setting his diamonds so that they caught up and cast back a multitude of lights. In so doing, he found it unnecessary to have an authorial voice gloss a scene. The brilliance floods in upon the reader; there is no necessity for Nick Carraway to say, as he did at one point in the pencil draft: "I told myself that I was studying it all like a philosopher, a sociologist, that there was a unity here that I could grasp after or would be able to grasp in a minute, a new facet, elemental and profound." The distance Fitzgerald traveled from *This Side of Paradise* and *The Beautiful and Damned* to *The Great Gatsby* is in the rewriting of the novel. There the sociologist and philosopher were at last controlled and the writer assumed full command.

III

Rewriting was important to Fitzgerald because, like many other good writers, he had to see his material assume its form — not in the *idea* of a character or a situation — but in the way character and situation and all the rest got down on paper. Once set down, they began to shape everything else in the novel, began to raise the endless questions of emphasis, balance, direction, unity, impact.

The whole of Chapter II in the finished novel (Chapter III in the draft) is an illustration of how the material took on its final form. That chapter begins with Dr. T. J. Eckleburg's eyes brooding over the ash heaps and culminates in the quarrel in Myrtle's apartment where "making a short deft movement, Tom Buchanan broke her nose with his open hand." Arthur Mizener first pointed out that the powerful symbol introduced in this chapter — Dr.

Eckleburg's eyes—was the result of Fitzgerald's seeing a dust jacket portraying Daisy's eyes brooding over an amusement park world. "For Christ's sake," he wrote to Perkins, "don't give anyone that jacket you're saving for me. I've written it into the book."[6] The pencil draft indicates that the chapter—marked Chapter III in the manuscript—was written at a different period of time from that of the earlier chapters. The consecutive numbering of the first sixty-two pages of the novel (the first two chapters) shows that for a long time Fitzgerald intended Chapter II as it now stands in the novel to be the third chapter.

In substance, the chapter remained much the same in the finished novel as it was in the draft. But, in addition to moving the chapter forward, Fitzgerald transposed to the next chapter a four-page section at the end describing Nick's activities later in the summer. Summing up Nick's character at the end of the third chapter gave more point to his concluding remark: "I am one of the few honest ["decent" in the draft] people that I have ever known" (p. 60). Bringing the Eckleburg chapter forward meant that the reader could never travel to or from Gatsby's house without traversing the valley of ashes. And ending the second chapter where it now ends meant that the reader could never get to Gatsby's blue gardens where "men and girls came and went like moths among the whisperings and the champagne and the stars" without waking up waiting for a four o'clock train in Penn Station.

But putting a brilliant chapter in place was only part of the task Fitzgerald could see needed to be done once the material was down on paper. Within that chapter, Fitzgerald's pencil was busily doing its vital work. The substance was all there: Tom and Myrtle and Nick going up to New York, the buying of the dog, the drinking in the apartment, the vapid conversations between the McKees and sister Catherine and Myrtle, the final violence. But some little things were not. The gray old man with the basket of dogs did not look like John D. Rockefeller until Fitzgerald penciled it in between lines; the mongrel "undoubtedly had Airedale blood" until Fitzgerald made it "an Airedale concerned in it somewhere"; and finally, the pastoral image of Fifth Avenue on a summer Sunday—"I wouldn't have been surprised to see a great flock of white sheep turn the corner"—this didn't arrive until the galleys.

---

[6] *The Far Side of Paradise* p. 170. The entire letter is to be found in *Letters*, pp. 165–167.

IV

The appearances of Gatsby, as might be expected, are among the most worked-over sections in the draft. Even when the manuscript was submitted, the characterization was not quite satisfactory, either to Fitzgerald or to Maxwell Perkins. The "old sport" phrase which fixes Gatsby as precisely as his gorgeous pink rag of a suit is to be found in only one section of the pencil draft, though it must have been incorporated fully into his speech before Fitzgerald sent off the manuscript. "Couldn't you add one or two characteristics like the use of that phrase 'old sport'—not verbal, but physical ones, perhaps," Perkins suggested.[7] Fitzgerald chose the most elusive of physical characteristics—Gatsby's smile. How he worked it up into a powerfully suggestive bit of characterization can be seen by comparing the pencil draft and the final copy. Gatsby is telling Nick about his experiences during the war:

Rough Draft	*Final Version*

"I was promoted to be a major/ and every Allied government gave me a decoration—/even ~~Bul~~ Montenegro little Montenegro down on the Adriatic/Sea!"
~~He lifted up the w~~ Little Montenegro! He lifted up the
            them
words/and nodded at ~~it~~ with a faint smile. My incredulity had/ had turned to facination now; ~~Gatsby was no longer a~~ it was/ ~~person he was a magazine I had~~ ~~picked up on the casually train~~
        like
~~and I was~~ reading the climaxes of
        only
all the stories/~~it contained~~ in a magazine.
	"I was promoted to be a major, and every Allied government gave me a decoration— even Montenegro, little Montenegro down on the Adriatic Sea!"
	    Little Montenegro! He lifted up the words and nodded at them —with his smile. The smile comprehended Montenegro's troubled history and sympathized with the brave struggles of the Montenegrin people. It appreciated fully the chain of national circumstances which had elicited this tribute from Montenegro's warm little heart. My incredulity was submerged in fascination now; it was like skimming hastily through a dozen magazines. (pp. 66–67)

[7] *Editor to Author: The Letters of Maxwell E. Perkins,* ed. John Hall Wheelock (New York, 1950), p. 39.

The smile is described in even fuller detail in a substantial addition to galley 15 (page 48 of the novel). One can virtually see Fitzgerald striking upon the smile as a characteristic which could give Gatsby substance without destroying his necessary insubstantiality.

Gatsby is revised, not so much into a real person as into a mythical one; what he *is* is not allowed to distract the reader from what he stands for. Without emphasizing the particulars of Gatsby's past, Fitzgerald wanted to place him more squarely before the reader.[8] Many of the further changes made in the galley proofs were directed toward that end. In the first five chapters of the galleys, the changes are the expected ones: routine corrections, happy changes in wording or phrasing, a few deletions, some additions. But at Chapter VI the galley proofs become fat with whole paragraphs and pages pasted in. Whole galleys are crossed out as the easiest way to make the extensive changes Fitzgerald felt were necessary. Throughout this section, he cut passages, tightened dialogue, reduced explicit statements in order to heighten the evocative power of his prose.

The major structural change brought the true story of Gatsby's past out of Chapter VIII and placed it at the beginning of Chapter VI. Chapter V, the meeting between Gatsby and Daisy, was already at the precise center of the novel.[9] That scene is the most static in the book. For a moment, after the confusion of the meeting, the rain, and his own doubts, Gatsby holds past and present together. The revision of Chapter VI, as if to prolong this scene in the reader's mind, leaves the narrative, shifts the scene to the reporter inquiring about Gatsby, and fills in Gatsby's real past. "I take advantage of this short halt," Nick Carraway says, "while Gatsby, so to speak, caught his breath" (p. 102). The deliberate pause illustrates the care with which the novel is constructed. The Gatsby of his self-created present is contrasted with the Gatsby of his real past, and the moment prolonged before the narrative moves on. The rest of Chapter VI focuses on the first moment of disillusion, Gatsby's peculiar establishment seen through Daisy's eyes.

---

[8] Fitzgerald wrote in response to Perkins's criticism: "His [Gatsby's] vagueness I can repair by *making more pointed* — this doesn't sound good but wait and see. It'll make him clear." In a subsequent letter, he wrote: ". . .Gatsby sticks in my heart. I had him for awhile, then lost him, and now I know I have him again" (*Letters,* pp. 170, 173).

[9] Fitzgerald called this chapter his "favorite of all" ("To Maxwell Perkins," *circa* Dec. 1, 1924, *Letters,* p. 170).

The rewriting so extensive in this chapter is as important as the shifting of material. The draft at this point has five different sets of numbers, and these pieces are fitted only loosely together. The Gatsby who finally emerges from the rewritten galleys answers the criticisms made by Maxwell Perkins and, more important, satisfies Fitzgerald's own critical sense. "ACTION IS CHARACTER," Fitzgerald wrote in his notes for *The Last Tycoon*. His revisions of dialogue, through which the novel often makes its vital disclosures and confrontations, shows his adherence to that precept. The truth of Gatsby's connection with Oxford was originally revealed to Nick Carraway in a somewhat flat, overly detailed conversation in which Gatsby tries to define his feeling for Daisy. Most of that conversation was cut out and the Oxford material worked into the taut dialogue between Tom Buchanan and Gatsby in the Plaza Hotel which prefaces the sweep of the story to its final action.[10]

In the draft, Gatsby reveals his sentimentality directly; he even sings a poor song he had composed as a boy. In the novel, a long passage of this sort is swept away, a good deal of the dialogue is put into exposition, and the effect is preserved by Nick's comment at the end: "Through all he said, even through his appalling sentimentality. . . ." (p. 112). In the draft, Gatsby carefully explains to Nick why he cannot run away. "'I've got to,' he announced with conviction, 'that's what I've got to do—live the past over again.'" Substance and dialogue are cleared away here, but the key idea is kept, held for a better place, and then shaped supremely right, as a climactic statement in a later talk with Nick: "'Can't repeat the past?' he cried incredulously. 'Why of course you can!'" (p. 111). In the draft, much of Gatsby's story is told in dialogue as he talks to Nick. It permits him to talk too much, to say, for example: "'Jay Gatsby!' he cried suddenly in a ringing voice. 'There goes the great Jay Gatsby! That's what people are going to say—wait and see.'" In the novel even the allusion to the title is excised. Gatsby's past is compressed into three pages of swift exposition punctuated by the images of his Platonic self,

[10] Mizener points out that Fitzgerald was revising almost up to the day of publication. The revision of this section came some time around February 18, 1925, when Fitzgerald cabled Maxwell Perkins: "Hold Up Galley Forty For Big Change" (*The Far Side of Paradise,* p. 164; p. 335, n. 63). Fitzgerald returned the proofs about February 18th. In a letter to Perkins, he listed what he had done: "1) I've brought Gatsby to life. 2) I've accounted for his money. 3) I've fixed up the two weak chapters (VI and VII). 4) I've improved his first party. 5) I've broken up his long narrative in Chapter VIII" (*Letters,* p. 177).

of his serving "a vast, vulgar, and meretricious beauty," and of Dan Cody and "the savage violence of the frontier brothel and saloon" from which he had come. Finally, in the draft, the undercurrent of passion and heat and boredom which sweeps all of them to the showdown in the Plaza is almost lost. Instead of going directly to the Plaza that fierce afternoon, they all went out to the Polo Grounds and sat through a ball game.

Of the changes in substance in this section—and in the novel—the most interesting is the dropping of a passage in which Gatsby reveals to Nick that Daisy wants them to run away. Daisy, elsewhere in the draft, reveals the same intentions. Perhaps Fitzgerald felt this shifted too much responsibility upon Daisy and made Gatsby more passive than he already was. Or perhaps his cutting here was part of a general intention of making Daisy less guilty of any chargeable wrong. Earlier in the draft, Fitzgerald removed a number of references to a previous romance between Daisy and Nick, and at other points he excised uncomplimentary remarks. The result may be contrary to expectation—that a writer ordinarily reworks to more sharply delineate a character—but it was not contrary to Fitzgerald's extraordinary intention. Daisy moves away from actuality into an idea existing in Gatsby's mind and ultimately to a kind of abstract beauty corrupted and corrupting in taking on material form.

V

After Chapter VI and the first part of Chapter VII, to judge both from the draft and the galleys, the writing seemed to go easier. The description of the accident with its tense climax—"her left breast was swinging loose like a flap"—is in the novel almost exactly as in the pencil draft. "I *want* Myrtle Wilson's breast ripped off"—he wrote to Perkins, "it's exactly the thing, I think, and I don't want to chop up the good scenes by too much tinkering."[11] Wilson and his vengeance needed little reworking, and though the funeral scene is improved in small ways, as is the conversation with Gatsby's father, no great changes occur here. The last ten pages, the epilogue in which Nick decides to go back West, are much the same, too.

In these last pages, as in the rest of the manuscript, one can

[11] *Letters,* p. 175.

only guess at how much writing preceded the version Fitzgerald kept as the pencil draft. "What I cut out of it both physically and emotionally," he wrote later, "would make another novel!"[12] The differences in hand, in numbering of pages, in the paper and pencils used, suggest that much had preceded that draft. Few of the pages have the look of Fitzgerald's hand putting first thoughts to paper, and fewer still—except those obviously recopied—are free of the revision in word and line which shows the craftsman at work.

These marks of Fitzgerald at work, the revelation they give of his ear and his eye and his mind forcing language to do more than it will willingly do, run all through the manuscript.

The best way of summarizing what Fitzgerald did in shaping *The Great Gatsby* from pencil draft to galley to book is to take him at his word in the introduction he wrote in 1934 for the Modern Library edition of the novel. "I had just re-read Conrad's preface to *The Nigger,* and I had recently been kidded half hay-wire by critics who felt that my material was such as to preclude all dealing with mature persons in a mature world. But, my God! it was my material, and it was all I had to deal with." What he did with it was what Conrad called for in his Preface, fashioned a work which carried "its justification in every line," and which "through an unremitting, never-discouraged care for the shape and ring of sentences" aspired to "the magic suggestiveness of music."

---

[12] Introduction to Modern Library edition of *The Great Gatsby* (New York, 1934), p. x.

J. Albert Robbins

Fitzgerald and the Simple, Inarticulate Farmer

It is the general impression that F. Scott Fitzgerald was too much
the literary playboy to read widely and thoughtfully but one of his
letters, written in 1925 to Maxwell Perkins, demonstrates a wide
and ready familiarity with modern literature as well as thought
upon the proper role of American fiction in his time.

The letter concerns the current novel of a younger novelist,
Thomas Boyd, whom the Fitzgeralds had met in St. Paul in 1921,
and whose first novel, *Through the Wheat* (1923), Fitzgerald had
badgered Perkins into accepting for publication by Scribner's.
At the time of this letter Fitzgerald had published *The Great
Gatsby* and was impatiently awaiting the critical verdict. Early in
May of 1925 Perkins wrote that Boyd's third novel, in process of
publication, was excellent. Soon thereafter he described the novel
in considerable detail and Fitzgerald's long letter of June 1, 1925,
contained his explosive reaction.

His letter is perhaps not so much a personal attack upon Boyd
as it was a release of tensions over the fate of *Gatsby;* frustration
and indignation with a reading public which buys romanticized,
escapist novels about struggling farmers; and pique that Perkins,
whose judgment and taste he respected, was susceptible also.
Clearly, Fitzgerald had been thinking about the proper subject
and role of the modern novel, and beyond doubt he felt it the
duty of the novelist accurately to deal with immediate realities

Reprinted from Modern Fiction Studies, *VII (Winter 1961–1962), 365–369,
by permission.* © *1961, by Purdue Research Foundation, Lafayette,
Indiana.*

rather than with reworked, superannuated materials. The basic issue is whether the novel dealing with the past, the novel celebrating the earthy struggle between man and the soil, is any longer central to the America of the twenties. Fitzgerald's answer is a definite and clear No, and he proceeds to document his position.

Before we turn to his views on the subject, it may be helpful to examine the nature of *Samuel Drummond* (1925), Boyd's forgotten novel of farm life which triggered Fitzgerald's assault. Drummond is the son of a substantial farmer in northwestern Ohio who grows to maturity just before the Civil War, marries, and settles down to a lifetime of hard work on his own farm near the family homestead. The father is a too-outspoken pacifist and his lack of enthusiasm for the northern cause brings on a visitation by enraged neighbors who, after brief fisticuffs, are persuaded to leave without further violence. As the war progresses, the son, Samuel, increasingly feels the pressure of local opinion and at last volunteers for military service. After Samuel's war experiences, which Boyd does not narrate, there commences the long and never-successful effort to revive a run-down farm. Samuel borrows money, and the debts which he cannot surmount eventually force him to sell his farm and face the monotony of an inactive life in a nearby town.

The dreary events which constitute the novel and the unimaginative, colorless characters who people it never save the story from mediocrity; and Fitzgerald is right in sensing that the novel exists basically to sentimentalize the plight of the honest but mindless farmer—just as he is right that it has all been said before. From the moment of their marriage Samuel and his bride are plunged into the ceaseless routines of household and field, where each year is like the last and the passage of time told only by the growth of offspring. Fitzgerald is right, too, in spotting the stereotype of inarticulateness—the muscular man of toil with the big heart and the minuscule vocabulary. At Drummond's wedding, Boyd notes, "Conversation was an art which was practiced with the greatest economy." Such a glorification of mindlessness implied a "greater truth" to be had from the virtues of labor and closeness to soil, but the reader is never led to see it. Although there are a few books in the Drummond house—Plutarch, Robert Burns, one or two Waverley novels, and a Bible—no one has time for them. "In the evenings." Boyd confesses, "they sat about the stove, talking little, waiting until it was time for them to go to bed." The inarticulateness and the sentimentality are underscored by the entry of a hired man, Christy, into the Drummond routine. On the way back from town one day Drummond picks up and gives shelter to this wanderer, who stays on for years as hired help—a homeless vagrant with no past whose rare moments of self-expression consist of such declarations as "I'm dumned if I would" and such exclamations as "Well, I'll be starched!" Christy, who is so artlessly injected into the novel, is as artlessly removed. One dark night, years later, he disappears and passes silently out of the Drummonds' lives.

In his letter, after vigorously disposing of a current rumor that he is about to forsake Scribner's for another publisher, Fitzgerald turns to the topic which occupies the larger part of his letter.[1]

> As you know despite my admiration for *Through the Wheat,* I haven't an enormous faith in Tom Boyd either as a personality or an artist—as I have, say, in E. E. Cummings and Hemmingway. His ignorance, his presumptuous intolerance and his careless grossness which he cultivates for vitality as a man might nurse along a dandelion with the hope that it would turn out to be an onion, have always annoyed me. Like Rascoe he has never been known to refuse an invitation from his social superiors—or to fail to pan these with all the venom of a James-Oliver-Curwood-He-Man when no invitations were forthcoming.
>
> All this is preparatory to saying that his new book sounds utterly lowsy—Shiela Kaye-Smith has used the stuff about the farmer having girls instead of boys and being broken up about it. The characters you mention have every one, become stock-props in the last ten years—"Christy, the quaint old hired man" after a season in such stuff as Owen Davis' *Ice Bound* must be almost ready for the burlesque circuit.
>
> *History of the Simple Inarticulate Farmer and his Hired Man*
> *Christy*
> (Both guaranteed to be utterly full of the Feel of the Soil)
> *1st Period*
> 1855—English Peasant discovered by Geo. Elliot in *Mill on the Floss,*
> *Silas Marner,* ect.
> 1888—Given intellectual interpretation by Hardy in *Jude* and *Tess*
> 1890—Found in France by Zola in *Germinal*

---

[1] The letter dated "6/1/25, 14 Rue de Tilsitt, Paris, France, is in the files of Charles Scribner's Sons, who have graciously provided me with a photocopy. I am grateful to Mrs. Frances S. F. Lanahan for permission to use this portion of the letter, the copyright of which is recorded in her name.

I have left Fitzgerald's misspellings uncorrected and unnoted, and have made an unimportant deletion in one sentence. The scholar will discover that Fitzgerald's memory for dates is faulty, but correct dates can readily be ascertained.

1900—Crowds of Scandanaivans, Hamsun, Bojer, ect, tear him bodily from the Russian, and after a peep at Hardy, Hamlin Garland finds him in the middle west.

———

Most of that, however, was literature. It was something pulled by the individual out of life and only partly with the aid of models in other literatures.

2nd Period

1914—Shiela Kaye-Smith frankly imitates Hardy, produces two good books and then begins to imitate herself

1915—Brett Young discovers him in the coal country

1916—Robert Frost discovers him in New England

1917—Sherwood Anderson discovers him in Ohio

1918—Willa Cather turns him Swede

1920—Eugene O'Niell puts him on the boards in *Different* and *Beyond Horizon*

1922—Ruth Suckow *gets* in before the door closes

These people were all good second raters (except Anderson). Each of them brought something to the business—but they exhausted the ground, the type was set. All was over.

———

3rd Period

The Cheapskates discover him—Bad critics and novelists, ect.

1923—Homer Croy writes *West of the Water Tower*

1924—Edna Ferber turns from her flip Jewish saleswoman[2] for a strong silent earthy carrot grower and the Great Soul of Charley Towne thrills to her passionately Real and Earthy Struggle

1924—*Ice Bound* by the author of *Millie the Beautiful Cloak Model* wins Pulitzer Prize

The Able McGloughlins [*The Able McLaughlins,* 1923, by Margaret Wilson] *wins $10,000 prize and is forgotten the following wk.*

1925—*The Apple of the Eye* [Glenway Wescott's first novel] pronounced a masterpiece

1926—TOM, BOYD, WRITES, NOVEL, ABOUT, INARTICULATE, FARMER WHO, IS, CLOSE, TO SOIL, AND, HIS, HIRED, MAN CHRISTY!

"STRONG! VITAL! REAL!"

As a matter of fact the American peasant as "real" material scarcely exists. He is scarcely 10% of the population, isn't bound to the soil at all as the English and Russian peasants were—and if has any sensitivity whatsoever (except a most sentimental conception of himself, which our writers persistently shut their eyes to, he is in the towns be-

---

[2] Emma McChesney, heroine of a series of short stories.

fore he's twenty. Either Lewis, Lardner and myself have been badly fooled, or else using him as typical American material is simply *a stubborn seeking for the static, in a world that for almost a hundred years has simply not been static.* Isn't it a 4th rate imagination that can find only that old property farmer in all this amazing time and land? And anything that ten people a year can do well enough to pass muster has become so easy that it isn't worth the doing.

I can not disassociate a man from his work.—That this Wescott . . . and Tom Boyd and Burton Rascoe . . . are going to tell us mere superficial "craftsmen" like Hergeshiemer, Wharton, Tarkington and me about the Great Beautiful Appreciation they have of the Great Beautiful life of the Manure Wielder—rather turns my stomach. The real people like Gertrude Stein (with whom I've talked) and Conrad (see his essay on James) have a respect for people whose materials may not touch theirs *at a single point.* But the fourth rate & highly derivative people like Tom are loud in their outcry against any subject matter that doesn't come out of the old, old bag which their betters have used and thrown away.

For example there is an impression among the thoughtless (including Tom) that Sherwood Anderson is a man of profound ideas who is "handicapped by his inarticulateness." As a matter of fact Anderson is a man of practically no ideas—*but he is one of the very best and finest writers in the English language today.* God, he can write! Tom could never get such rhythms in his life as there are on the pages of *Winesburg, Ohio*—Simple! The words on the lips of critics makes me hilarious. Anderson's style is about as simple as an engine room full of dynamoes. But Tom flatters himself that he can sit down for five months and by dressing up a few heart throbs in overalls produce literature.

It amazes me, Max, to see you with your discernment and your fine intelligence fall for that whole complicated fake. Your chief critical flaw is to confuse mere earnestness with artistic sincerity. On two of Ring's jackets have been statements that he never wrote a dishonest word (maybe it's one jacket). But Ring and many of the very greatest artists have written thousands of words in plays, poems and novels which weren't even faintly sincere or earnest and were yet *artisticly sincere.* The latter term is *not* a synonym for plodding ernestness. Zola did not say the last word about literature, nor the first.

I append all the data on my fall book, and in closing I apologize for seeming impassioned about Tom and his work when neither the man or what he writes has ever been personally inimical to me. He is simply the scapegoat for the mood Rascoe has put me in and, tho I mean every word of it, I probably wouldn't have wasted all this paper on a book that won't sell & will be dead in a month & an imitating school that will be dead by its own weight in a year or so, if the news about Liveright hadn't come on top of the Rascoe review[3] and ruined my disposition.

It is at once apparent that Fitzgerald has loaded his argument and has indiscriminately mingled mature use of the rural (Frost and Cather, for example) with the shallow and sentimental use of it (Ferber and Boyd, for example), but he was drawing upon memory and general knowledge and writing in heat and haste. Yet, Fitzgerald perceives the anomaly in the fact that the farm novel has particularly flourished at the peak of American urbanization and industrialization, and that it has been presented repeatedly in sentimental, not in realistic, terms.[4]

The one recent novel of the type which Fitzgerald selects for emphasis is a superb example, for Edna Ferber's *So Big* was both true to the type and immensely popular. Selina, a school teacher, marries a man of the soil. The farmer-husband, who appears so fleetingly in the novel, is an inarticulate, near-illiterate but handsome giant of a man who stirs Selina to such raptures as "The dear thing! The great helpless big thing!" Once widowed, Selina assumes her husband's tasks, triumphs over the inevitable odds against her, and senses her noble service to humanity by providing wholesome food for the great city of Chicago, food that "keeps people's bodies clean and clear and flexible and strong!" Fitzgerald had seen the rave review by Charles Hanson Towne, who in the April, 1924, *Literary Digest International Book Review* had called Miss Ferber "the biggest novelist we have in this country" and had affirmed that "there is not a sentence . . .that is not literature."

Basically Fitzgerald's critical instincts were right. Time has indeed upheld Cummings and "Hemminway," and has rather roughly handled such novels as *West of the Water Tower* and such creations as Samuel Drummond's hired man, Christy.

[3] It is difficult to say what review Fitzgerald had in mind. It is possible that he is referring to the review of *The Great Gatsby* in the April 19, 1925, issue of *The New York Herald and Tribune Books,* where the novel was called "a book of the season only"—but Rascoe had resigned as literary editor of the newspaper the previous year.

[4] For a scholar's view of this matter, see John T. Flanagan, "The Middle Western Farm Novel," *Minnesota History,* XXIII (June, 1942), 113–125.

Arthur Mizener

Scott Fitzgerald and the 1920's

There is a very obvious pitfall that yawns before anyone who undertakes to talk about an author and his period, a pitfall that is no less dangerous for being obvious. Imaginative writers are not historians, and the better they are—no matter how representative —the less they resemble historians. They have in them little or none of the generalizing and quantifying impulse of historians because they do not know the world as a play of something called forces and tendency on things called groups and classes. Imaginative writers know their experience of the world, not an abstraction from it, and know that experience symbolically, not logically. There is nothing mysterious about this process; it is the way we all know our experience a great deal of the time, so that every time we begin a story by saying, "a funny thing happened to me today," or "wait till I tell you about. . . ," we are doing, in our humble way, what the imaginative writer does. That is, we are finding a particular person acting in a particular way at a specific time and place significant of something beyond himself. It is worth repeating the "funny thing that happened today" only because that thing embodies a meaning for us, a meaning that may, when the person who tells the story is a gifted man, give us an understanding of our time different from the historian's but complementary to it and—in some respects, at least—more revealing.

Scott Fitzgerald had an imaginative sense of the experience of the 1920's, was indeed a writer so closely related to his time that he was in danger of being wholly absorbed by his sense of it and of

Reprinted from the Minnesota Review, *I (Winter 1961), 161–174, by permission of the author.*

writing books that would not survive it. But if you are not careful to make clear that in saying this you do not mean his work is history in the usual sense, you are sure to land in trouble. I have almost never touched on this aspect of Fitzgerald's work without having someone in the audience rise after the lecture to say that he personally lived through the 1920's without ever wearing a coonskin coat, reading *The American Mercury,* hearing Paul Whiteman, or entering a speakeasy. Certainly hundreds of thousands of people—the vast majority of Americans, in fact—did. Of course Fitzgerald's work tells us nothing about the 1920's in this sense. But one might as well argue that Shakespeare's plays tell us nothing about Elizabethan England because Hamlet was a Dane, Macbeth a Scotsman, and Lear, if anything historical at all, God alone knows what.

The meaningful question to ask of Fitzgerald's work is how much it reveals about the quality of his time, the movement of attitude and feeling in it; how much it penetrates to meaning and motive, that is, in the period, however statistically unrepresentative may be the specific particulars it selects from the period to convey this understanding. These things, too, are a kind of history, perhaps the essential kind of history, and of it Fitzgerald's sense was extremely acute. Whatever he was writing about and whatever his other interests in it, he was always aware of what it suggested about his time and place. Thus he will remark in passing:

> By 1927 a wide-spread neurosis began to be evident, faintly signalled, like a nervous beating of the feet, by the popularity of crossword puzzles. I remember a fellow expatriate opening a letter from a mutual friend of ours, urging him to come home and be revitalized by the hardy, bracing qualities of the native soil. It was a strong letter and it affected us both deeply, until we noticed that it was headed from a nerve sanitarium in Pennsylvania.

In an important sense, there is more history in that paragraph than there is in all the conventional social histories of the 1920's put together, even though Fitzgerald is ostensibly talking about a statistically minute minority of Americans—the intellectuals of the period—and about only three of them, none of whom is, in the full sense, even in America, since two of them are expatriates living on the Riviera and one is in an insane asylum.

The advantage of such an imaginative grasp of life is that it can look at a time and a place and see past the normative statistical formulas, the pious falsehoods, and that exercise of a tenth-rate poetic faculty called the advertising business that produces what it likes itself to call "The Image" of America. I do not mean that even a fine imagination is always right; far from it. No doubt, in fact, the egg-head view of America is as frequently wrong as the mutton-head view. But right or wrong, it is always concerned to reach through the appearances of things to their essences—not, of course, as Mr. Tate has told us in *The Forlorn Demon*—directly, but indirectly. I suppose the way the imagination oftenest goes wrong in the ordinary sense is by becoming subject to the distortions imposed by its private experience, for it is ultimately always alone with itself, can never "prove" anything, even to itself.

What it does know, however, it knows as experience. Fitzgerald's favorite poet, Keats, felt the importance of this kind of knowledge so strongly that, as he said in a famous letter to Benjamin Bailey, he had "never yet been able to perceive how anything can be known for truth by consecutive reason." Because he had never been able to, he cried out for a life of "Sensations"—that is, the felt understanding of the imagination—rather than "Thoughts"—the logical conclusions of consecutive reasoning. That is why he said that "what the imagination seizes as beauty—that is, *experienced* knowledge—must be true." Fitzgerald loved Keats as he did because he too had that conviction.

It is the astonishing flowering of the imagination in this sense during the American 20's—most strikingly no doubt in our poetry, but in our prose too—that justifies our special interest in the period, however silly some of the manifestations of that interest in the popular press may be. America had had its great writers before the 20's. In fact, it had had four or five in the nineteenth century who were probably greater writers than any of those who appeared in the 1920's—at least this is, I believe, so of the prose writers. But writers like Hawthorne and Melville and James were isolated giants—isolated not simply from their society but even from the society of their fellows. We know the pathetic and unsuccessful effort of Melville to reach an understanding with Hawthorne; we know the artificiality of the relation between Emerson and Whitman; we know the pitiful failure of Thoreau's famous call on Whitman; we know Henry James's remark to the group in Edith Wharton's drawing room at Lenox, after he had read aloud a poem of Whitman's: "One cannot but deplore his knowledge of foreign languages"; perhaps most pathetic of all, we know that Melville and Whitman lived quite near each other for years without, so far as we know, ever meeting at all.

The result was that though the imaginations of these men were undoubtedly profoundly affected by their times, they achieved no common sense of them and could never deal directly with them. This is still a problem for the American writer, so that there is a sense in which our best prose writers are often still producing, not novels but philosophical romances—which for all I know is a greater form than the novel, but does not do one important thing the novel does do, that is, present a verisimilar image of its world. Hawthorne and Melville certainly wrote romances, fictions that are located at a distance of time or place from their own world; James may be a more arguable case, but I think he did too. At least when Ford Madox Ford, in his large, easy way, asserted that there was a period of his boyhood that he "passed very largely in Paris, and very largely in exactly the same society as that in which Newman himself moved," people laughed at him, quite rightly, since there never was—as Henry James clearly recognizes in the preface to *The American*—any such society. *The American* is a romance. So, surely, are most of Faulkner's novels. But if this difficulty in dealing directly with the author's world still bothers American fiction, it is clearly not the problem it once was, and it is not, I think, because in the 1920's there was a sudden flourishing of talented young men in America who popped up all over the country, filled with a common conviction that it was possible to produce serious works of the imagination directly about American experience. Moreover, these young men quickly found one another and formed that loose, anarchic, strife-torn society that still constitutes the intellectual community of our time—intellectual underground, perhaps I should call it. There are lots of neat, superficial little historical and sociological explanations of this odd flowering—many of them produced for public lectures by members of the intellectual community itself: intellectuals will of course try on any idea for size. None of them is, I think, to be trusted very far. We really haven't the faintest idea why this miracle occurred. But whatever the reason for it, it produced something very different in the way of a literature than had been produced by the lonely giants of the nineteenth century.

When William James urged his brother Henry to stay in America and write about that wonderful product of democratic American society, The New Man, Henry went off to live in England and to write about its cultivated upperclass life, for reasons he made quite clear in his life of Hawthorne. The best he could do for William was to create the hero of *The American,* a fellow called

Newman; Newman did not satisfy William at all. But Fitzgerald and Hemingway and Dos Passos and Cozzens and the rest could not have been persuaded not to write about The New Man and his society, though I doubt if William James would have been pleased by *their* vision of him either. They clearly felt what always seems to be felt by writers in periods of great imaginative activity; they seemed to themselves to have suddenly been released from some invisible restraint, to have been made free to discover and reveal the private truth about American experience. Even Sinclair Lewis clearly felt this, though his sense of the private truth of American experience was sentimental and crude. Lewis's strength was a Mencken-like feeling for the absurdity of the public and conventional American life of his time, of the world so admired by *Time Magazine.*

It was no doubt a dramatic and exciting time in America, the 20's, and that may have had something to do with the feelings of these young men. The shift of power from Europe to America that took place after the first world war was bound to excite any imagination capable of grasping it at all. As Fitzgerald put it in his characteristic way,

> With Americans ordering suits by the gross in London, the Bond Street tailors perforce agreed to moderate their cut to the American long-waisted figure and loose-fitting taste, [and] something subtle passed to America, the style of man.

Moreover, it was a period that ran its course rapidly and excitingly. Fitzgerald said afterwards that it lasted almost exactly ten years, beginning with the May Day riots of 1919 "when the police rode down the demobilized country boys gaping at the orators in Madison Square" and leaping, as he put it, "to a spectacular death in October, 1929."

What it felt like to be living through the early days of that decade is most beautifully realized in one of the finest of Fitzgerald's early stories, "May Day." Of the so-called "May Day riots" described with such wonderful irony in that story, Fitzgerald said elsewhere that "we didn't remember anything about the Bill of Rights until Mencken began plugging it, but we did know that such tyranny belonged in the jittery little countries of south Europe. If goose-livered business men had this effect on the government, then maybe we had gone to war for J. P. Morgan's loans after all."

This feeling made two courses possible, and they were both

followed in the period. These young people with their optimistic belief that the good life was possible in this new and powerful America could either fight to make America what they thought it ought to be or they could—and it was easy in a wealthy period—retire into a small world of their own where they might live as they pleased and let the booboisie go its own benighted way. There were people like Walter Lippmann and Heywood Broun—and, in part, Mencken—who followed the first course, but the majority—"tired," as Fitzgerald said, "of Great Causes" and alienated by the kind of small-town pettiness that could imagine Prohibition a Great Cause—followed the second course. Mencken is such a key figure for the period because he did both, and did so with a kind of gross and ebullient wit that makes him peculiarly appealing to Americans.

He liked to say, when asked to lecture to Women's Clubs, "I am seldom out of Baltimore, and when I am, I am never out of my cups." When he was confronted by that favorite witticism of the stupid, "If you do not like America why do you live in it?" he would say, "Why do men go to zoos?" This was the way intelligent young people, staring confidently out from the privacy of their little world, saw the absurd public and ordinary life of America.

They did so with very considerable political courage and honesty. The fact that they were libertarians interested in private freedom rather than in public equality as liberals are, and that they hardly participated in organized political movements until the Sacco-Vanzetti case in 1927, ought not to blind us to their impertinent defiance of the ruling powers. Mencken was a master of such impertinence, calling the President of the United States, Calvin Coolidge, "the heir of Washington, Lincoln, and Chester A. Arthur," and describing the average well-behaved 101% Rotarian business man as someone "who goes to bed every night with an uneasy feeling that there is a burglar under the bed, and gets up every morning with a sickening fear that his underwear has been stolen."

When William Jennings Bryan—the idol of those Americans who disapproved of all new ideas, including the one Bryan fought so energetically at the Scopes trial, namely, evolution—when Bryan died, Mencken wrote an obituary of him for the Baltimore *Sun* that begins, "Has it been duly marked by historians that the late William Jennings Bryan's last secular act on this globe of sin was to catch flies?" and goes on to observe of Bryan that,

For forty years he tracked [Homo neandertalensis] with coo and bellow, up and down the rustic backways of the Republic. Whenever the flambeaux of Chatauqua smoked and guttered, and the bilge of idealism ran in the veins . . . and men gathered who were weary and heavy laden and their wives who were full of Peruna and as fecund as shad—there the indefatigable Jennings set up his traps and spread his bait. He knew every country town in the South and West, and he could crowd the most remote of them to suffocation by simply winding his horn.

Thus Mencken talked about Calvin Coolidge, the President of the United States, and Bryan, its dignified ex-secretary of State. If you will try to imagine anyone talking today in this way about President Eisenhower and Secretary Dulles you will have some measure of Mencken's political impertinence and courage.

He talked the same way about issues. In the midst of the Palmer Red Raids, one of those periodic displays of childish hysteria about communism that we Americans regularly disgrace ourselves with, Mencken wrote,

Let a lone Red arise to annoy a barroom full of Michigan lumberjacks, and at once the fire-alarm sounds and the full military and naval power of the nation is summoned to put down the outrage. But how many Americans would the Reds convert to their rubbish, even supposing them free to spout it on every street corner? Probably not enough, all told, to make a day's hunting for a regiment of militia. The American moron's mind simply doesn't run in that direction; he wants to keep his Ford even at the cost of losing the Bill of Rights.

There is a gift here, amounting almost to a kind of genius, for insulting all the conceivable sacred cows of American society at once. But behind Mencken's delight in stirring up the animals there is a serious attitude that was common to the intelligent young people of his time. It is made up of a love of personal freedom and a respect for the rights of individuals, however wrong one may think them, of a dislike of doctrinaire egalitarianism and a respect for superior intelligence and talent, however annoying it may be, of a dislike of the complacent vulgarity of the majority and the politicians and advertisers who pander to and encourage it and a respect for intellectual dissatisfaction and the artists who represent it.

This, then, was the way the public world looked to the cultivated, young people of the American 20's. Most of them, in the early 20's at least, saw little hope of changing it and felt little impulse to try, though more of them became interested in politics toward the end of the period. Most of them stayed inside their little underground community and there tried and—alas, because it was in many ways an admirably conceived ambition—failed to live the good life. Occasionally—Fitzgerald was a great one for this kind of thing—they made a serio-comic foray into the world of conventional behavior and newspapers in order to say boo to the Babbitts, but mostly they stayed within their own world. Looking back at it afterwards, Zelda Fitzgerald said with her sharp insight and her slightly schizoid wit,

> "We're having some people," everybody said to everybody else, "and we want you to join us," and they said, "We'll telephone." All over New York people telephoned. They telephoned from one hotel to another to people on other parties that they couldn't get there—that they were engaged. It was always teatime or late at night.

And Fitzgerald himself said,

> It was borrowed time anyhow—the whole upper tenth of a nation living with the insouciance of grand ducs and the casualness of chorus girls. But moralizing is easy now and it was pleasant to be in one's twenties in such a certain and unworried time. . . . Sometimes . . . there is a ghostly rumble among the drums, an asthmatic whisper in the trombones that swings me back into the early twenties when we drank wood alcohol and every day in every way grew better and better, and there was a first abortive shortening of the skirts, and girls all looked alike in sweater dresses, and people you didn't want to know said "Yes, we have no bananas," and it seemed only a question of a few years before the older people would step aside and let the world be run by those who saw things as they were—and it all seemed rosy and romantic to us who were young then, because we will never feel quite so intensely about our surroundings any more.

Keatsian romantic that he was, Fitzgerald could never deny the kind of truth that intensity gave, and that is why, of all this brilliant group of writers in the 20's who were bent on showing—in Hemingway's phrase—exactly "the way it was" in that time of hope and promise, Fitzgerald was most acutely aware of the way it was.

All these writers were romantics of one kind or another, as perhaps all Americans must be, but Fitzgerald was by temperament the special kind of romantic that Keats also was, and he therefore felt with special poignancy, just as Keats did, the irony

of time. He lived, as Malcolm Cowley once put it, in a room full
of clocks and calendars. Small wonder that he borrowed a phrase
from Keats's "Ode to a Nightingale" for the title of the novel in
which he described with loving hindsight the 20's defeated romantic dream of the good life, and called the book *Tender Is the Night*.
Or that the most brilliant passage he ever wrote about American
experience—the final paragraphs of *The Great Gatsby*—deals
with the romantic dilemma in exactly the same terms, and in
almost as complex a figure, as do the famous opening lines of
Keats's "Ode on a Grecian Urn."

Precisely because he so loved the products of time in all their
mortal and evanescent glory, Fitzgerald longed to have them last
forever, unchanged, just as Keats longed to believe that he could
remain "awake for ever in a sweet unrest" "Pillow'd upon my fair
love's ripening breast." Both knew that they could not, that even
the *foster* child of silence and slow time, the Grecian urn that was
not even truly eternal, achieved its merely relative permanence
at the cost of being incapable of the very thing they wished to make
permanent, what Keats called "the wild ecstasy," the passion and
intensity of a realized love.

The dilemma is familiar enough to western culture. It was
by no means a recent poet, even as the history of literature goes,
who remarked that,

> When I have seen by time's fell hand defaced
> The rich proud cost of outworn buried age . . .
> Ruin hath taught me thus to ruminate—
> That time will come and take my love away.

Fitzgerald's wry, twentieth-century version of this feeling was:
"It grows harder to write, because there is much less weather than
when I was a boy and practically no men and women at all."

But the remarkable thing about Fitzgerald is that he was not
a historian, even of ideas; he was a poet, a man who experienced
this idea, felt it anew and as if no one had ever experienced it
before, and felt it therefore wholly in terms of the world *he* lived
in. By doing so, he displayed, unintentionally, and as the result
of an accident that made his experience representative, one of the
distinguishing characteristics of the American sensibility, one of
the attitudes that do make us new men in western culture, if a very
different kind of new men from those William James thought he
saw. Do we not feel that one of the characteristic polarities of the

American consciousness is that between an intense idealism, an extravagant vision of the good life, and a passion for the actual and concrete? Men with a passion for the actual and concrete are usually willing to settle for limited goods that can be realized here and now; politics, they say, is the art of the possible. Idealists are likely to put the realization of their ideals into the remote future, when the state will wither away, etc., in order not to have to face the impossibility of realizing them here and now. But the American imagination seems to combine a powerful idealism with a passion for the actual, and, indeed, the peculiarly American actual. It is this insistence on having both the dream and its realization that makes Jay Gatsby's life tragic, and no less so because he is innocently unaware of how much he is asking for. It is also what made Scott Fitzgerald's life tragic. It is, indeed, the source of tragedy for American life in general.

There is a wonderful intuitive grasp of this fact about us in Fitzgerald's making his most important hero a man of provincial American origin, an almost Horatio Alger young man from a Middlewestern farm named James Gatz, who has what Fitzgerald calls "a heightened sensitivity to the promises of life" and is determined to the point of dying for it to realize these promises in an actual marriage with the novel's heroine, Daisy Fay. Neither the realities of time nor the contingencies of human character discourage him. When he discovers that in the five years since he has last seen Daisy Fay she has married and had a child, Gatsby decides that he will take her back to Louisville to the place—*and* the time, he obviously believes—where they had left off, and that they will start their life over again from there. "I wouldn't ask too much of her," Fitzgerald's narrator says to him. "You can't repeat the past." "Can't repeat the past?" Gatsby cries incredulously, "Why, of course you can!" And when he is finally driven to admit that Daisy may have loved her husband, as he says, "just for a minute, when they were first married"—an enormous concession for him— he immediately adds, "In any case, it was just personal."

Like the hero he imagined as the embodiment of the romantic's "heightened sensitivity to the promises of life," the world he imagined those promises conceived in and defeated by is the world he—and all of us—actually experiences them in. Fitzgerald understood the essential act of Keats's imagination so well precisely because he had experienced it independently, not in the world of nightingales, of "green hills in an April shroud," of "globèd peonies," but in a world where the full glory of nature is known as Nick Carraway knows it in *The Great Gatsby* when he suddenly becomes conscious that "it was deep summer on roadhouse roofs and in front of wayside garages, where new red gas pumps sat out in pools of light." If Wordsworth, looking once again, after five years absence, at the countryside a few miles above Tintern Abbey will say with intense excitement that once again he sees "these pastoral farms, / Green to the very door," Nick Carraway will know the same feeling of excitement by contemplating a Long Island estate where "the lawn started at the beach and ran toward the front door for a quarter of a mile, jumping over sun-dials and brick walks and burning gardens—finally when it reached the house drifting up the side in bright vines as though from the momentum of its run."

No wonder Fitzgerald understood—indeed, had felt himself—what Gatsby feels about Daisy Fay's house in Louisville, that

> There was a ripe mystery about it, a hint of bedrooms upstairs more beautiful and cool than other bedrooms, of gay and radiant activities taking place through its corridors, and of romances that were not musty and laid away already in lavender but fresh and breathing and redolent of this year's shining motor cars and of dances whose flowers were scarcely withered.

This was a luxurious house, because Daisy Fay's family was wealthy. This fact is crucial to an understanding of Fitzgerald and of the 20's he represented, and I want in conclusion to examine it and even to argue that the attitude Fitzgerald and the 20's took toward wealth is a more honest one than we allow ourselves today, and perhaps the only one that will justify the life of the richest country in the world, insofar as that country lives up to any ideal and can be justified at all.

The first thing that has to be recognized is that, though Fitzgerald's imagination was much preoccupied by wealth, he was almost completely uninterested in it for its own sake, just as he was deeply scornful of rich people who were merely rich, feeling about them, as he said, "not the conviction of a revolutionist [that makes one think he can improve things] but the smouldering hatred of a peasant [that assures one he cannot]." Beautiful as Daisy Fay was, most things about her were faintly disappointing to Gatsby when he met her again after dreaming about her for nearly five years, for almost "no amount of fire and freshness," as Fitzgerald puts it, "can challenge what a man can store up in his ghostly heart." The only thing about Daisy that does not thus slightly fail Gatsby is her voice with its "inexhaustible charm," a charm that has been cultivated, refined, and preserved by the conditions of her whole life, the circumstances that have surrounded her because she has lived always in the luxurious world of wealth. "Her voice," says Gatsby suddenly, like a man blurting out the unmentionable secret of all our lives, "is full of money." The money means nothing in itself; the last thing Gatsby loves is money. What he loves is the full realization of the natural beauty of Daisy's voice and—as he mistakenly believes—of all the rest of her nature that has been made possible by wealth.

This is what Fitzgerald's imagination grasped about American life, that wealth is enormously important to it because as American society is constituted—just possibly as any society is constituted—only wealth provides the conditions that make the full realization of life's promises possible, and that a preoccupation with material possessions is justified only when those possessions are used for the realization of the finest life an imagination of heightened sensitivity can conceive. This is almost exactly the inverse of George Orwell's lifelong argument that the essential virtues are simply not possible in a life of grinding poverty, and there is perhaps something characteristic in the fact that Eton's great secular moralist dwelt characteristically on the evils of poverty and Princeton's on the promises of wealth.

We Americans seem to suffer under a peculiar taboo about wealth. By some kind of conspiracy of silence, we work together to persuade ourselves that we think what we call "beautiful *homes*" —perhaps because they are so often only houses—clubs, schools, universities, cars, clothes, all of which, heaven knows, cost a great deal of money, are nice enough but not necessary to our virtue and happiness. Almost pathetically, for a business civilization, we even cling to the pretense that wealth is not the foundation of social position. Fitzgerald's imagination was somehow freed from this taboo; he recognized clearly, and did not even know he was not supposed to say, that the rich are different from you and me—and luckier in the possibilities of their lives. Thus he was able to perceive without confusion all there was to know about the subtle and complex structure of sentiment and attitude we build up almost from birth around objects and activities that are conspicuously expensive. He understood completely our feelings for cars, for resort hotels, for interior decoration and antiques, for what we ambiguously call "the best" colleges and universities. He can make us laugh in a very special way at his schoolboy hero, Basil Duke Lee, lounging—as he says—"passionately" behind the wheel of a Stutz Bearcat, because he knows that he is making us laugh at a secret passion of our own. There is a whole aspect of American culture to be defined in terms of our never-forgotten youthful feelings about a car, especially as that car is associated with social prestige and with our first experiences of love.

Fitzgerald's imagination, with its American impulse to fix on the concrete and actual, understood supremely well how close our feelings cling to the objects with which they were associated when they were most intense—to the cars, the clothes, the country-club or college dances, the popular tunes so expensively played on those occasions. He understood that we must face honestly the fact that the great good place we can imagine is a place that requires money for its existence.

He was not strikingly optimistic about the prospect of our not being damned by our materialism, of our dream's surviving its entanglement with particularly expensive objects. Who was ever so damned, finally, as Daisy Fay, whom Gatsby dreamed of as his golden princess high in a white tower? All the beautiful people of Fitzgerald's stories are damned in one way or another. But damned or not, Fitzgerald's imagination told him, we live along the lines of that web of feelings we have woven around what he once called "the appurtenances of happiness," the expensive physical objects with which all our feelings are identified. Which one of us, if he is quite honest with himself, does not know that the sources of our secret emotional lives are in the unforgotten triumphs and griefs of our youth and that our dream of happiness is, however sophisticated, always a version of what Fitzgerald once described in a little ballad:

> There'd be an orchestra
>   Bingo! Bango!
> Playing for us
>   To dance the tango,
> And people would clap
>   When we arose,
> At her sweet face
>   And my new clothes.

Whether it is good or bad to be this kind of people—and I suppose it is both—we are indeed something like that. And it is Fitzgerald's true greatness as a writer that he helped his age—and therefore us—to see that this was "the way it was."

William E. Doherty

Tender Is the Night *and*
the "Ode to a Nightingale"

Critics often express a feeling that there is something mysterious about Fitzgerald's *Tender Is the Night,* that there is something unsatisfying in the analyses we have had—a discomfort one does not feel with the more elaborately structured *The Great Gatsby,* or with the intriguing, unfinished *The Last Tycoon.* Searching the critical opinion on *Tender Is the Night*—this "magnificent failure" —one is likely to feel that something *is* missing; one seems to have, as Maxwell Geismar says, "the curious impression at times that the novel is really about something else altogether."[1]

It seems strange that the relationship between the novel and Keats's "Ode to a Nightingale," which supplied Fitzgerald with both title and epigraph, should have received no more than passing attention from the critics. The epigraph reads:

> Already with thee! tender is the night,
> . . .
> But here there is no light,
> Save what from heaven is with the breezes blown
> Through verdurous glooms and winding mossy ways.

We know that Fitzgerald had a lifelong and deep response to Keats: "for awhile after you quit Keats all other poetry seems to

---

[1] Maxwell Geismar, *The Last of the Provincials,* (Cambridge, Mass., 1947), 333.

Reprinted from Explorations of Literature, *ed. Rima Drell Reck, copyright Louisiana State University Press, 1966, by permission of the publisher.*

be only whistling or humming." The "Ode to a Nightingale" was especially important to him; he found it unbearably beautiful, confessed he read it always with tears in his eyes.[2]

I

It is true that the title *Tender Is the Night* was chosen late in the extended course of the book's writing; but it seems clear that Fitzgerald was conscious of the "Ode" not merely in the last stages of composition. The title is appropriate, though no one has said why. Yet, a moment's reflection will show that there is a good deal of Keatsian suggestiveness in *Tender Is the Night* in both decor and atmosphere—the Provençal summers of sunburnt mirth, the nights perfumed and promising, the dark gardens of an illusory world. But I suggest that there are parallels more significant than those of color and mood. The correspondences I offer in this case, when taken individually, might seem no more than coincidental; but considered in their cumulative weight, they indicate a calculated pattern of allusion beneath the literal surface of the novel which deepens the psychoanalytic rationale and adds context to the cultural analysis the book offers. In addition, the "Ode" appears to provide us with a sort of thematic overlay which clarifies unsuspected symbolic structures, essential to the understanding of the book.

I will begin with an admission that weakens my case. Fitzgerald dropped a reference to the nightingale from his second and subsequent versions of the published novel. In the *Scribner's Magazine* version he wrote of "roses and the nightingales" that had become an essential part of the beauty of that "proud gay land," Provence.[3] Why that observation was dropped, I cannot say; but its appearance, however brief, suggests that like Keats, Fitzgerald associated the south of France with the romantic bird. There is a second and more interesting reference which remained. It too connects the bird and the south of France. To understand its significance, one must consider it in context.

The Riviera, Mediterranean France, came to be, as Maxwell Geismar has pointed out, that apogee of ease and grace, that "psychological Eden" in which Fitzgerald and his heroes took

[2] F. Scott Fitzgerald, *The Crack-up* (New York, 1956), 298.
[3] F. Scott Fitzgerald, "Tender Is the Night, a Romance," *Scribner's Magazine,* XCV (January-June, 1934), 7.

refuge.[4] None of his characters responds more fully to this environment than does Rosemary, coming as she does from the "salacious improvisations of the frontier." At the party at the Villa Diana, no guest is more enchanted by the life that seems promised there; she feels a sense of homecoming, feels drawn as if by magnetic lights. The spell of the party is still on her as she lies awake in her room "suspended in the moonshine . . . cloaked by the erotic darkness." She is disturbed by secret noises in the night: an "insistent bird" sings in the tree outside. She is not sure what bird it is, but the singing and the Divers seem to merge in her mind: "Beyond the inky sea and far up that high, black shadow of a hill lived the Divers. She thought of them both together, heard them still singing faintly a song like rising smoke, like a hymn, very remote in time and far away."[5] But Rosemary is confused by it all; she cannot think as yet except through her mother's mind. Abe North identifies the bird for her:

> "What are *you* doing up?" he demanded.
> "I just got up." She started to laugh. . . .
> "Probably plagued by the nightingale," Abe suggested and repeated, "probably plagued by the nightingale" (42).

The entire chapter, heavy with night imagery, seems to lead up to this identification. Rosemary has been brought up with the idea of work. Now she is on a summer's holiday, an emotionally lush interval between two winters of reality; and what she discovers is a world remote, romantic, something southern, a mysterious dark lure of life to which she responds—symbolized by the night bird. It is unreal; a duel will be fought; "up north the true world thundered by."

What I suggest is that the novel deals with characters who are plagued by the nightingale, those enamored of the romantic illusion. Nicole seems to be the nightingale.

Consider the scene in which Nicole sings to Dick. As she waits for Dick at the sanatorium, singing surrounds Nicole, summer songs of ardent skies and wild shade. The night, the woods, gardens, flowers are associated with Nicole throughout the novel. Here, the unknown seems to yield her up, "as if this were the exact moment when she was coming from a wood into the clear moon-

---

[4] Geismar, 290–291.

[5] F. Scott Fitzgerald, *Tender Is the Night* (New York, 1962), 40. Quotations in the text are from this edition unless otherwise indicated.

light" (135). Dick responds to that illusion, wishes that she had no other background, "no address save the night from which she had come." She leads him to a secret copse. In this melodious plot she has hidden a phonograph. She plays for him "thin tunes, holding lost times and future hopes in liaison." Through song the two of them are transported out of the copse into another world. The journey is chronicled in ironic song titles. Finally Nicole herself sings to Dick. She supposes he has heard all these songs before. "'Honestly, you don't understand—I haven't heard a thing.' Nor known, nor smelt, nor tasted, he might have added" (136). Now here was this girl bringing him the essence of a continent, "making him a profound promise of herself for so little. . . . Minute by minute the sweetness drained down into her out of the willow trees, out of the dark world" (136). But there is danger in the promise of this "waif of disaster," in the song of this "young bird with wings crushed."

The brief transport from the world which the "Ode" details, the emotional adventure of climax and decline is suggested in this and in a number of other scenes in *Tender Is the Night.* Indeed, the pattern describes the very rhythm of the novel. The party at the Villa Diana, as Malcolm Cowley suggests, appears to be the high point in the story. The scene marks a change of mood; thereafter, the light romantic atmosphere is dispelled.[6] We see there the Divers at their point of greatest charm—a "vision of ease and grace," commanding all the delicacies of existence. It is a high point for another reason. It is in this scene that the principals of the story make an escape from the prosaic and temporal world. In the rarefied atmosphere of the party a moment is caught in which a delicate triumph over time is achieved.

The party is given out-of-doors in the garden, Nicole's garden. To Rosemary the setting seems to be the center of the world: "On such a stage some memorable thing was sure to happen" (29). The guests arrive under a spell, bringing with them the excitement of the night. Dick now seems to serve Nicole as prop man, arranging the set, dressing the trees with lamps. The guests are seated at Nicole's table:

There were fireflies riding on the dark air and a dog baying on some low and far-away ledge of the cliff. The table seemed to have risen a little toward the sky like a mechanical dancing platform, giving

[6] Malcolm Cowley, "Introduction," *Tender Is the Night* (New York, 1956), *xvii.*

the people around it a sense of being alone with each other in the
dark universe, nourished by its only food, warmed by its only lights.
And, as if a curious hushed laugh from Mrs. McKisco were a signal
that such a detachment from the world had been attained, the two
Divers began suddenly to warm and glow and expand, as if to make
up to their guests, already so subtly assured of their importance, so
flattered with politeness, for anything they might still miss from that
country well left behind. Just for a moment they seemed to speak to
everyone at the table, singly and together, assuring them of their
friendliness, their affection. And for a moment the faces turned up
toward them were like the faces of poor children at a Christmas tree.
Then abruptly the table broke up—the moment when the guests had
been daringly lifted above conviviality into the rarer atmosphere of
sentiment, was over before it could be irreverently breathed, before
they had half realized it was there.

But the diffused magic of the hot sweet South had withdrawn
into them—the soft-pawed night and the ghostly wash of the Mediterranean far below—the magic left these things and melted into the
two Divers and became part of them (34–35).

When we consider the care with which Fitzgerald dresses this
scene, we sense an emphasis beyond what the mere events of the
party would demand. This garden, the fireflies riding on the dark
air, the summer evening, the wine-colored lanterns hung in the
trees—the Romantic decor is there, and the Keatsian atmosphere:
"the diffused magic of the hot sweet South . . . the soft-pawed
night and the ghostly wash of the Mediterranean far below. . . ."
There is no need to insist that these images have their antecedents
in the "Ode"—in its "murmurous haunt of flies on summer eves,"
or its "warm south," its "tender night," its "charmed magic case-
ments opening on perilous seas"; for the clearest parallel to the
poem lies in the brief achievement of the precious atmosphere,
achieved through the familiar Romantic formula of escape at the
moment of emotional pitch—here ironically, a moment of social
ecstasy, but suggesting inevitably the dynamics of the sexual event.
The imagery itself reiterates the pattern: the fragile loveliness of
Nicole's garden increases "until, as if the scherzo of color could
reach no further intensity, it broke off suddenly in mid-air, and
moist steps went down to a level five feet below" (26).

It seems unlikely that the material of the "Ode" was so immediate in Fitzgerald's mind that it would come to add to the novel a
dimension of allusion of which he was unaware. We are willing to
concede unlimited conscious subtlety to his contemporaries in the
novel; but Fitzgerald, despite the evidence of his deliberate work-

manship, is too often pictured by critics as a somewhat fatuous tool of the muse, whose mind was inferior to his talent. The intricacies of *Tender Is the Night* would suggest otherwise. Not only is the pattern of the momentary climax a repeated one in the novel; there occurs, too, the *recall to reality* that marks the ending of the "Ode." In the novel it is not the sound of a bell that signals the descent from bliss—or the word "forlorn" striking like a bell, tolling the poet back to his sole self; it is another sound heard three times in the book: when Dick falls in love with Nicole, when Abe leaves on the train from Paris, and when Tommy becomes Nicole's lover. Each time a shot is heard, a loud report that breaks the illusion signifies the end of happiness and the escape from self.

After Nicole leaves the sanatorium, Dick tries to avoid her; but she fills his dreams. Their chance meeting in the Alps ends in Dick's complete surrender of self: "he was thankful to have an existence at all, if only as a reflection in her wet eyes" (155). As in all her love situations, Nicole is triumphant, self-controlled, cool: "I've got him, he's mine" (155). The scene remains tender; it is raining, the appropriate weather for love in Fitzgerald's novels. But, "suddenly there was a booming from the wine slopes across the lake; cannons were shooting at hail-bearing clouds in order to break them. The lights of the promenade went off, went on again. Then the storm came swiftly . . . with it came a dark, frightening sky and savage filaments of lightning and world-splitting thunder, while ragged, destroying clouds fled along past the hotel. Mountains and lakes disappeared—the hotel crouched amid tumult, chaos and darkness" (155–56).

This is not the storm of passion. Dick has come suddenly to his senses: "For Doctor Diver to marry a mental patient? How did it happen? Where did it begin?" The moment of passion and illusion is over. He laughs derisively. *"Big* chance—oh, yes. My God!—they decided to buy a doctor? Well, they better stick to whoever they've got in Chicago" (156). But Dick has committed himself to Nicole. His clear sight comes too late, and when the storm is over her beauty enters his room "rustling ghostlike through the curtains."

A loud shot sounds the ominous recall another time, in the Paris railway station. Here is departure and farewell; a gunshot cracks the air. Abe, on the train, waves good-bye, unaware of what has happened. The shots do not mark the end of his happiness, for he has long been in misery, though they do forebode his violent death. It is the brief summer happiness of Dick—won in a desperate bargain with the gods—that is ending. It marks the end of a summer mirth for the Divers' group, the beginning of misfortune for Dick. Dick and his friends move out of the station into the street as if nothing had happened. "However, everything had happened—Abe's departure and Mary's impending departure for Salzburg this afternoon had ended the time in Paris. Or perhaps the shots, the concussions that had finished God knew what dark matter, had terminated it. The shots had entered into all their lives. . ." (85).

The third of these recalls to reality occurs just after Tommy possesses Nicole. The entire account from the arrival of Tommy at the Villa Diana to the departure from the hotel presents a curious parallel to the ending of the "Ode." Tommy comes to Nicole like a worshiper before a mystery. His happiness intensifies: "And, my God, I have never been so happy as I am this minute" (294). But the time of joy is brief; the point of greatest happiness is a moment outside of self, a taste of oblivion. The ecstasy passes; disappointment and foreboding follow: "The nameless fear which precedes all emotions, joyous or sorrowful, inevitable as a hum of thunder precedes a storm." After the act, things begin to look tawdry to Tommy. He is edgy and apprehensive. Outside there are disturbing noises: "There's that noise again. My God, has there been a murder?" The final recall is heard. As they leave the room "a sound split the air outside: Cr-ACK-Boom-M-m-m! It was the battleship sounding a recall. Now, down below their window, it was pandemonium indeed. . ." (296–97). There is a rush to depart. Cries and tears are heard as the women shout farewells to the departing launch. The last ludicrous moments of the scene, the girls shouting their tearful good-byes from the balcony of Tommy's room, waving their underwear like flags, appear to be Fitzgerald's ironic counterpart to the adieu of the final stanza of the poem. The fading anthem of the "Ode" becomes the American National Anthem: "Oh, say can you see the tender color of remembered flesh?—while at the stern of the battleship arose in rivalry the Star-Spangled Banner" (297).

II

The title of the novel and the epigraph Fitzgerald offers illuminate the significance of "night" and "darkness" in the story. An enquiry reveals a complicated and careful symbolic structure in *Tender Is the Night* involving a contrast between the night and the day, darkness and light. The title of the novel declares that the night is tender. There is in it an implicit corollary about the day.

Early in the story, the sun is established as something harsh and painful, even maddening. The sun troubles the Divers and their group. They seek shelter from it under their umbrellas which "filter" its rays. At the beach the sea yields up its colors to the "brutal sunshine." Rosemary retreats from the "hot light" on the sand. Dick promises her a hat to protect her from the sun and to "save her reason." In the scene in which Nicole lapses into madness at the Agiri Fair, "a high sun with a face traced on it beat fierce on the straw hats of the children." The day scenes are those of pain and fear: "the April sun shone pink upon the saintly face of Augustine, the cook, and blue on the butcher's knife she waved in her drunken hand" (265).

On the other hand, darkness and the night are addressed in fond, in honorific terms: "the lovely night," the "soft rolling night," the "soft-pawed night," the "erotic darkness." Fitzgerald's description of Amiens reveals something of the character and virtue of the night: "In the daytime one is deflated by such towns . . . and the very weather seems to have a quality of the past, faded weather like that of old photographs. But after dark all that is most satisfactory in French life swims back into the picture—the sprightly tarts, the men arguing with a hundred Voilas in the cafés, the couples drifting, head to head, toward the satisfactory inexpensiveness of nowhere" (59). Part of the meaning is here, but the symbolism of the night is not merely opposite in meaning to that of the day; it is more complicated and more intricately woven into the story. The night is the time of enchantment, masking the ugliness of reality that the day exposes. The night, as in the "Ode," is the time of beauty and the time of illusion. Dick and his friends prefer the night: "All of them began to laugh spontaneously because they knew it was still last night while the people in the streets had the delusion that it was bright hot morning" (79). But the night is not entirely superior to the day. The desirable night is the all allowing darkness. It is a dimness preferred, perhaps, by those ineffective in dealing with the practical day-lit reality. If the day is harsh, it has vigor; the night is the time of ease and also weakness. Some hint of these sinister implications may be detected in the scene in which Baby Warren makes her frustrated effort to aid Dick after he has been beaten and thrown into the Roman jail. She cannot function in the real world: "She began to race against the day; sometimes on the broad avenues she gained but whenever the thing that was pushing up paused for a moment, gusts of wind blew here and there impatiently and the slow creep of light began once more" (227). She cringes at the unstable balance between night and day. The strange creature she encounters in the embassy, wrapped and bandaged for sleep, "vivid but dead," appears an unwholesome figure of the night, incongruous with the day.

It would appear that Fitzgerald has divided his world into two parts—the night and the day. The day is reality, hard, harsh, and vigorous; the night is illusion, tender, joyful, but devitalizing.

The most significant illusion that the night fosters is the illusion of happiness. To the Romantic, happiness consists in preserving the high moment of joy. He has a dread of endings. *Tender Is the Night* is a book of endings: "Things are over down here," says Dick. "I want it to die violently instead of fading out sentimentally" (37–38). Paradoxically, the Romantic dream is that the moment of joy can be embalmed forever in the final night; death then appears to be a welcome extenuation of the night, ending all endings. Both the poem and the novel deal with these lovely illusions; but what they teach is that the fancy cannot cheat so well, that disillusionment is the coefficient of time.

There is a difference in tone between the two works which is due to the fact that Keats emphasizes the swelling dimension of the ecstatic experience, while Fitzgerald deals more with its deflation. Where Keats conveys a sense of disappointment, fond regret, Fitzgerald expresses a Romantic's anti-Romantic argument; for in tracing the grim disenchantment Fitzgerald underscores the sense of deception, trickery, the sense of victimage in the martyring of the dreamer. The "immortal bird" of the "Ode" becomes the "perverse phoenix" Nicole; the deceiving elf becomes the "crooked" Nicole, one of a long line of deceivers, pretending to have a mystery: "I've gone back to my true self," she tells Tommy; ". . . I'm a crook by heritage" (292). We suspect complicity in her father's sin; he tells the doctor, "She used to sing to me" (129).

There are other victims of the Romantic deception—the inmates of the sanatorium where Dick labors without accomplishment. "I am here as a symbol of something" (185), the American woman artist tells Dick. She and the others are there because "life is too tough a game" for them. Unlike the thick-ankled peasants who can take the punishment of the world on every inch of flesh and spirit, these are the fine-spun people suffering private illusions, their "compasses depolarized." They are "sunk in eternal darkness," people of the night, spirits sensitive and weak, now caught in Nicole's garden. For it is Nicole who has designed the means of holding these inmates fast. With floral concealment and deceptive ornament she has created those camouflaged strong points in which they are kept. Outwardly these houses are attractive, even cheerful, screened by little copses; but "even the flowers lay in iron fingers." Perhaps the "Ode" suggested the names: the "Beeches" and the "Eglantine."

III

These inmates are, many of them, the "victims of drug and drink." There is in *Tender Is the Night* what might be called a potion motif, involving liquor, drugs, and poison. As in the "Ode" these are associated with the illusory adventure. Dr. Diver is as much an addict as his patients. In the early parts of the novel, wine is associated with the delicacy of living the Divers maintain and with the sensual qualities of their lives. The enjoyable swim in the ocean is like the pleasure of "chilled white wine." The wine-colored lamps at the Villa Diana give a lively flush to Nicole's face. Nicole is gay-spirited after the "rosy wine at lunch." There is a faint spray of champagne on Rosemary's breath when Dick kisses her for the first time. But wine quickly loses its pleasant character. As Dick's esteemed control begins to slip and he acts for the first time without his customary "repose," he stares at the shelf of bottles, "the humbler poisons of France—bottles of Otard, Rhum St. James, Marie Brizzard. . . ." Dick's Roman debauch recalls Abe's disastrous drunks. At home Dick drinks brandy from a three-foot bottle. He comes to regard liquor as food, descending to the level of the rich ruins he treats. Late in the novel we see that the sinister qualities of these draughts, potions, beakersful are associated with Nicole: in falling in love with her, in marrying her, Dick "had chosen the sweet poison and drunk it." Again Nicole is characterized as the attractive evil, the sinister allurement.

The draught of vintage from the deep delved earth, the dull opiate, the hemlock of Keats's poem may not be the direct sources of Fitzgerald's images; yet the associations of drug, drink, and poison with the Romantic appetencies are interesting and suggest that Keats and Fitzgerald were dealing with a similar psychological syndrome—the urge to "fade away, dissolve and quite forget. . . ."

This urge, as Albert Guerard, Jr., points out in his essay,

"Prometheus and the Aeolian Lyre," is really the urge toward loss of self, the impulse toward self-immolation, to the drowning of consciousness—one of the hallmarks of the Romantic temperament—which accepts the myth of a vital correspondence between man and nature, a correspondence demanding the submersion of our rational, coherent selves. In the "Ode to a Nightingale," Mr. Guerard argues, Keats has written a poem about the actual submersion of consciousness, dramatizing the process itself, and presenting in the poem a symbolic evasion of the actual world:

> In one sense this ode is a dramatized contrasting of actuality and the world of the imagination, but the desire to attain this fretless imaginative world becomes at last a desire for reason's utter dissolution: a longing not for art but for free reverie of any kind. . . . This sole self from which Keats escapes at the beginning of the poem, and to which he returns at its close, is not merely the conscious intellect aware of life's weariness, fever, and fret, but truly the sole self: the self locked in drowsy numbness, the self conscious of its isolation. . . .[7]

Mr. Guerard's analysis may be modified, perhaps, to this degree: the "Ode" seems not so much a product of the Romantic myth of a prevailing correspondence between man and nature as it is an acknowledgment that the correspondence does not prevail. This thesis is reiterated in *Tender Is the Night*. What the nightingale symbolizes and promises in the "Ode," Nicole symbolizes and promises too. The ecstatic union with the bird is a taste of oblivion in loss of self.

Dick manifests the symptoms that Mr. Guerard indicates. There is the obsessive awareness of isolation that characterizes Dick even in his student days. He feels separated from his "fathers." He has the feeling that he is different from the rest, the isolation of the scientist and the artist—"good material for those who do most of the world's work"; but it is a loneliness he cannot endure. He wanted to be good, to be kind; he wanted to be brave and wise; but, as we learn toward the end, "he had wanted, even more than that, to be loved" (302). He gives a strange answer to Franz's criticism of his scholarship: "I am alone today. . . . But I may not be alone to-morrow" (138). One by one he burns his books to keep warm. In marrying Nicole he abandons his work in "effortless immobility." The critics have frequently noted the self-sacrificial aspect of Dick's behavior; but too frequently that self-sacrifice has been taken as the very theme of the novel because Dick gives himself so completely in serving others that he is left with nothing in the end. Rather, this self-sacrifice should be understood as one of the paradoxical impulses which constitute the desire to submerge the self. Self-immolation seems to contradict the longing for freedom from burdens and cares, yet both urges are aspects of the desire to abandon individuality. Abe, like Dick, has a strong desire for loss of self, and forgetfulness. Abe wants oblivion and seeks it in drink; he longs for death. Tommy too has inclinations toward the moribund, following death and violence all over the world. Baby Warren "relished the foretaste of death, prefigured by the catastrophes of friends" (172). Dick looks fondly at death in his decline. At the railing of Golding's yacht he comes close to suicide and to taking Nicole with him. The isolation Dick feels as a young man is never relieved. The entire age is alien to him. Dick mourns on the battlefields of World War I: "All my beautiful lovely safe world blew itself up here with a great gust of high explosive love" (57). Coming home to bury his father, he feels the final tie has been broken; there is no identity with his own land; he feels only a kinship with the dead: "Good-by, my father—good-by, all my fathers" (205).

IV

Finally, what does the correspondence between the novel and the "Ode" reveal about the social and cultural analysis Fitzgerald offers in *Tender Is the Night*? The distinction between the night and the day that Fitzgerald establishes symbolically has its significance in the "class struggle" he presents; the social antagonisms seem to be aspects of the antipathy which arises between the Romantic and the anti-Romantic disposition.

Fitzgerald, as we have seen, divides things into opposing pairs in *Tender Is the Night*. When Rosemary arrives at the Riviera beach she finds two groups. The McKisco party is made up of McKisco, the *arriviste* who has not yet arrived, his silly ambitious wife, two effeminates, and the shabby-eyed Mrs. Abrams. They are pale, gauche people, unattractive beside the Divers' group. The Divers are rich, cultured, talented, leisured. We get a fuller understanding of what these groups may represent in the scene in which

Dick and Rosemary visit the house on the Rue Monsieur. It is a place of incongruities and contrasts. Clearly there is a clash between the past and the present, suggesting, it seems, the evolving future of the Western world:

> It was a house hewn from the frame of Cardinal de Retz's palace in the Rue Monsieur, but once inside the door there was nothing of the past, nor of any present that Rosemary knew. The outer shell, the masonry, seemed rather to enclose the future so that it was an electric-like shock, a definite nervous experience, perverted as a breakfast of oatmeal and hashish, to cross that threshold. . ." (71).

The people within are an odd mixture. They fit awkwardly into the environment. They lack the command over life that earlier ages managed to exert. Rosemary has a detached "false and exalted feeling" of being on a movie set. No one knew what the room meant because it was evolving into something else. It is important to recognize who these people in the room are:

> These were of two sorts. There were the Americans and English who had been dissipating all spring and summer, so that now everything they did had a purely nervous inspiration. They were very quiet and lethargic at certain hours and then they exploded into sudden quarrels and breakdowns and seductions. The other class, who might be called the exploiters, was formed by the sponges, who were sober, serious people by comparison, with a purpose in life and no time for fooling. These kept their balance best in that environment, and what tone there was, beyond the apartment's novel organization of light values, came from them (72).

The room apparently holds the society of the West. We find in it the McKisco group, the sponges, the hard practical people; and there are the Divers' type, the dissipated old "quality" class, the run-down Romantics who are doomed. The sober and serious exploiters set the tone for the future, and in it they will succeed. Rosemary stands between the two groups. Her youth and success separate her from the Divers' crowd, but she inclines toward them by temperament and training. She is a product of her mother's rearing, tutored in the values of the old society. "I'm a romantic too," Rosemary tells Dick. Yet, she is coldly practical, "economically . . . a boy not a girl." The first day on the beach Rosemary does not know which group is hers. She is attracted by the Divers' party; but, "between the dark people and the light, Rosemary found room and spread out her peignoir on the sand" (5–6).

The people of the McKisco type are not the victims of Nicole; they are immune to the Romantic illusion. The "tough minded and perennially suspicious" cannot be charmed. McKisco is the only one at the party at the Villa Diana who remains unassimilated, unaffected by the emotional excursion. In the house on the Rue Monsieur there are others who are likewise immune. The "cobra women" discuss the Divers:

> "Oh, they give a good show," said one of them in a deep rich voice. "Practically the best show in Paris—I'd be the last one to deny that. But after all—" She sighed. "Those phrases he uses over and over—'Oldest inhabitant gnawed by rodents.' You laugh once."
> "I prefer people whose lives have more corrugated surfaces," said the second, "and I don't like her."
> "I've never really been able to get very excited about them, or their entourage either. Why, for example, the entirely liquid Mr. North?" (72–73).

The incapacity for illusion gives these people an advantage in the world. McKisco, for whom the sensual world does not exist, ends successful and honored; his novels are pastiches of the work of the best people of his time. "He was no fool about his capacities— he realized that he possessed more vitality than many men of superior talent, and he was resolved to enjoy the success he had earned" (205). McKisco's duel with Tommy symbolizes the clash between the two groups and underscores the anachronism of the soldier and hero. Tommy is a product of the older civilization, educated in forgotten values. Ironically it is McKisco who is "satisfied" in the duel. He builds a new self-respect from his inglorious performance. Tommy, Abe, and Dick are Romantic remnants, the children of another century, fettered by its illusions—"the illusions of eternal strength and health, and of the essential goodness of people; illusions of a nation, the lies of generations of frontier mothers who had to croon falsely, that there were no wolves outside the cabin door" (117).

They are the salt of the earth—charming, gifted people, but overmatched in the struggle against the cold, shrewd frauds who are inheriting the earth. *Tender Is the Night* deals with the passing of the old order, with the passing of an attitude toward life, or rather with the last remnants of that life, "the oldest inhabitants gnawed by rodents." The specific content of the illusions which fetter them is less important than how Fitzgerald deals with the attraction to the irrational dream which marks the romantic temperament, a dream which may promise the world, the sustained

ecstasy of love, or the satisfactions of oblivion—symbolized by
the beautiful, mad woman, Nicole. She is the dream without real
referent. She has no existence outside the mind of the dreamer:
"When I talk I say to myself that I am probably Dick. Already I
have even been my son, remembering how wise and slow he is.
Sometimes I am Doctor Dohmler and one time I may even be an
aspect of you, Tommy Barban. Tommy is in love with me . . ."
(162).

In the end it is Dr. Diver who is "cured" when he releases
her from his mind; he returns to the terrible emptiness of the
"sole self." Late in the novel Nicole sings to him again in her "harsh
sweet contralto." But this time Dick will not listen: "I don't like
that one" (290).

The dream and the dreamer are, of course, Fitzgerald's subject matter in fiction; and in treating them he invariably delivers
up the dreamer as victim of his own Romantic infatuations. And
yet for all his insight, his self-lacerating satire, Fitzgerald leaves
the dream and the dreamer somehow inviolable at the end.
Gatsby, that most extravagant Romantic, leaking sawdust at every
pore, is still intact at the end and dies with his dream intact. "No—
Gatsby turned out all right at the end; it was what preyed on
Gatsby, what foul dust floated in the wake of his dreams . . ." that
defeated him.

The best of the Romantic writers are not vulnerable to their
own myths. The "Ode to the Nightingale" declares exquisitely the
abandonment of faith in the imagination. It is not until *Tender Is
the Night* that Fitzgerald abandons that last comfort of the Romantic, the notion that the botching, the disappointment of the
imagination's most cherished ambitions may be blamed on the
unworthy environment of the dreamer. *Tender Is the Night* is a
harder, harsher book than *Gatsby;* and it tells us that the super-
dream is an internal corruption, a damaging, self-begotten beauty.
Dick's final return to his sole self in upstate New York—"almost
certainly in that section of the country, in one town or another"
—is an utterly unsentimental fade-out; the hero is gone from the
stage before we can cover him with our fond sympathy, before we
can murmur, "Alas."

Michael Millgate

The Last Tycoon

On 29 September, 1939, Fitzgerald wrote to his publisher that his new novel, *The Last Tycoon,* had been set "safely in a period of five years ago to obtain detachment."[43] A year later, in September 1940, we find him telling Gerald Murphy that the novel is "as detached from me as *Gatsby* was, in intent anyhow."[44] That final qualifying phrase raises doubts which the letterhead reinforces (Twentieth Century-Fox Film Corporation Studios, Beverly Hills, California),[45] and in fact the detachment seems to have proved elusive: *The Last Tycoon* lacks the distanced, curiously "classical" air of *The Great Gatsby.* The volume as we have it contains a collection of brilliant and powerful scenes; these hardly begin to cohere into a novel, and not only for the reason that the book was unfinished.

Indeed, we may doubt whether Fitzgerald could have finished *The Last Tycoon* according to his original conception. Many of Fitzgerald's difficulties derived from the fact that he was, in effect, writing two novels in one: a "psychological" novel about Monroe Stahr, and a "social" novel about Hollywood. In his letter to

[43] F. Scott Fitzgerald, Notes to *The Last Tycoon,* in *Three Novels of F. Scott Fitzgerald,* New York [1953], p. 141.

[44] *The Crack-Up,* ed. Edmund Wilson, New York [1945], p. 282.

[45] *Op. cit.,* p. 281.

Reprinted from American Social Fiction *(Edinburgh and London: Oliver & Boyd, 1964; New York: Barnes & Noble, 1965), by permission of the author. The article first appeared as "Scott Fitzgerald as Social Novelist: Statement and Technique in* The Last Tycoon," *English Studies, 43 (February, 1962), 29–34. Footnote numbers from the book publication have been retained.*

127

Edmund Wilson of 25 November, 1940, the emphasis appears to be on the latter: "I honestly hoped somebody else would write it [the novel] but nobody seems to be going to."[46] However, the starting-point of the book seems clearly to have been the genius of Stahr himself, "the last tycoon," just as the central interest of *The Great Gatsby* had been in Gatsby himself. The "social" interest in *The Great Gatsby,* though considerable, serves primarily to display and explain the human relationships: it never takes control. In *The Last Tycoon,* as far as it had gone, the "social" content also remains reasonably functional, but we may judge from Fitzgerald's plans for the conclusion of the novel that had he tried to work out the plot of *The Last Tycoon* along the lines he proposed, his growing interest in the intrigue, corruption and violence of Hollywood might well have taken control and swamped the rest.

Fitzgerald does not seem fully to have realized that in *The Last Tycoon* he faced a problem of construction quite different from the one he had so brilliantly solved in *The Great Gatsby;* otherwise he would surely not have tried to cast his new book so completely in the *Gatsby* mould. Since he planned *The Last Tycoon* as a short novel of about fifty-one thousand words, he turned naturally to *The Great Gatsby* for a usable pattern, and the frequent references to *The Great Gatsby* in Fitzgerald's notes for *The Last Tycoon* and in his letters at this time make it clear that while he was planning and writing the new book he had the earlier one very much in mind. In any case, this would have been sufficiently plain from a comparison of the two. Each tells the story of a man who, from humble beginnings, has risen to a position of great power. In each we first come to know of the man not in person but by reputation and by the attitude of others towards him. Then we see the man himself in the center of his world, his position and his greatness defined by the nature of that world which revolves upon him as its axis: Fitzgerald's outline for *The Last Tycoon* says explicitly that he intends the chapters describing Stahr's day to be "equal to guest list and Gatsby's party,"[47] namely, to Chapter Three and the first two pages of Chapter Four of *The Great Gatsby.* We watch in each the failure of the man in his personal life, in an all-important relationship with a woman; then his violent, senseless death; and finally his funeral, so strongly contrasted with his life (in notes for the end of *The Last Tycoon* Cecilia imagines Stahr present at the funeral and saying "Trash!").[48]

[46] *Op. cit.,* p. 285.
[47] Notes to *The Last Tycoon,* p. 142.
[48] *Op. cit.,* p. 132.

The most important and perhaps the most questionable of *The Last Tycoon's* debts to *The Great Gatsby* is the half-involved first-person narrator. Fitzgerald describes Cecilia as "*of* the movies but not *in* them";[49] a very similar comment could have been made about Nick Carraway's place in the world of *The Great Gatsby*. But Nick, as a piece of structural machinery, is a superb invention: he remains on stage almost throughout the novel, and we are never in doubt about the sources of his information. Nick as narrator never strains our credulity; Cecilia as narrator worries us from the start. Fitzgerald clearly intended her to play a Nick Carraway role, but because of her own limited participation in the action she cannot fulfill Nick's narrative function. Nick's other major role is to act as a vehicle for moral judgments, and here again Cecilia falls short. Fitzgerald planned a final scene in a sanatorium, intending to invest Cecilia, through her illness, with greater portentousness, but she lacks weight in the story as we have it. She seems too immature, and too involved emotionally with the people and actions she describes to be able to make worthwhile judgments or to help us to judge.

The correspondences between *The Last Tycoon* and *The Great Gatsby* are not accidental, and they may have helped to twist *The Last Tycoon* out of its proper path, whatever that may have been. Gatsby's violent death has ironic appropriateness, but the violent death proposed for Stahr seems unmotivated and relatively without point, except in so far as Fitzgerald was planning a reference back to the airliner episode in Chapter One. The unsatisfactory love-affair forms the core of *The Great Gatsby* and indeed of Gatsby himself, but, although Fitzgerald told his publisher that he wanted Stahr's affair with Kathleen to be "the meat of the book,"[50] he seems not to have had a completely clear conception of their relationship. In fact, Stahr the lover remains a somewhat shadowy figure in the chapters that we have, and it is certainly Stahr the producer and businessman who emerges the more vividly.

Because the making of motion-pictures involves questions of artistic judgment, it seems, as Fitzgerald noted, rather an odd kind of business. But it unquestionably is a business: as Cecilia Brady tells us on the first page, "My father was in the picture business as another man might be in cotton or steel."[51] The enmity

---

[49] *Op. cit.,* p. 138.
[50] *Op. cit.,* p. 139.
[51] *The Last Tycoon,* p. 3.

between Stahr and Brady derives largely from the latter's exclusively business approach to film-making, but Stahr himself, though he must pronounce on matters of taste, remains inevitably a businessman as well. When Wylie White challenges Stahr's description of himself as a "merchant," Stahr sticks to the word and suggests that Charles Francis Adams, when he criticized "Gould, Vanderbilt, Carnegie, Astor," was "'probably a sourbelly.' . . . 'He wanted to be head man himself, but he didn't have the judgment or else the character.'"[52]

Stahr thus seems to align himself with the great American capitalists. But the tone of his answer works together with Wylie White's admiration to prevent our thinking of him entirely in these terms, and when we see him at lunch with the financiers we quickly realize his isolation among them. As a young man he had been "more than now . . . a money man among money men. Then he had been able to figure costs in his head with a speed and accuracy that dazzled them."[53] Since then, we learn, Stahr "had grown away from that particular gift, though it was always there."[54] Stahr remains a brilliant businessman, but he has become something more. Fitzgerald's grand conception of Stahr both includes his business ability and transcends it:

> He spoke and waved back as the people streamed by in the darkness, looking, I suppose, a little like the Emperor and the Old Guard. There is no world so but it has its heroes, and Stahr was the hero. Most of these men had been here a long time—through the beginnings and the great upset, when sound came, and the three years of depression, he had seen that no harm came to them. The old loyalties were trembling now, there were clay feet everywhere; but still he was their man, the last of the princes. And their greeting was a sort of low cheer as they went by.[55]

The kind of representative importance with which Fitzgerald intended to invest Stahr does not wholly emerge in the novel as we have it. But it becomes sufficiently plain that if Stahr is an embodiment of heroic individualism he has—despite his paternalism, his dislike of unions, and his fight with Brimmer—nothing of the Fascist about him. Indeed, one of the major themes of *The Last Tycoon* seems to be a partial identification of Stahr with

[52] *Op. cit.,* pp. 16–17.
[53] *Op cit.,* p. 45.
[54] *Ibid.*
[55] *Op. cit.,* p. 27.

Abraham Lincoln. Arthur Mizener has pointed out the importance of the Lincoln motif in Fitzgerald's presentation of Stahr: he relates it, with the reference to Andrew Jackson in the episode at The Hermitage in the opening chapter, to the "political fable" Fitzgerald seems to have been developing in the book.[56] It may be, however, that the identification of Stahr with Lincoln, though never complete, goes further than this, affecting other sides of Stahr's character and other aspects of the book.

Boxley, the English novelist, finds Stahr irritating, but "he had been reading Lord Charnwood and he recognized that Stahr like Lincoln was a leader carrying on a long war on many fronts. . . . Stahr was an artist only, as Mr. Lincoln was a general, perforce and as a layman."[57] Going to Lord Charnwood's biography, *Abraham Lincoln,* it is interesting to discover Charnwood quoting contemporary references to Lincoln as "the Tycoon"[58] and as "King Abraham I."[59] The coincidence with Fitzgerald's title is striking, and usefully reminds us that Fitzgerald intended Stahr as a "tycoon" in the original sense of that word quite as much as in the modern sense. There seems a possible hint here, too, of Fitzgerald's description of Stahr as "the last of the princes" and of the moment when Kathleen assures Stahr that her real king was not nearly so king-like as Stahr himself.[60]

There are other points of similarity between Charnwood's Lincoln and Fitzgerald's Stahr: both are men of humble origins and little education but of great ability and vision; both practice in their relations with subordinates complete accessibility and an unforced personal democracy; both accept without hesitation the full responsibility of their position while disliking many of the duties involved. As Fitzgerald saw, an obvious analogy can be drawn between Stahr's position and Lincoln's: Stahr can be seen as the commander-in-chief, receiving reports from the battleline, issuing orders to his generals (the directors), overseeing work which has to be done in detail by others. In a smaller way, Lincoln's habit of telling a little story when a reproof had to be administered somewhat resembles Stahr's method of handling Boxley, while it is surely in terms of the Lincoln analogy that the curious scene with the Negro on the beach at Malibu begins to

[56] Arthur Mizener, *The Far Side of Paradise,* London 1951, pp. 295–6.
[57] *The Last Tycoon,* p. 106.
[58] Lord Charnwood, *Abraham Lincoln,* London 1917, p. 234.
[59] *Op. cit.,* p. 377.
[60] *The Last Tycoon,* p. 112.

take on fuller meaning: like Lincoln, but unlike Wylie White earlier in *The Last Tycoon,* Stahr will transform his kingdom for the Negro's sake.

Above all, Stahr resembles Lincoln in responding supremely to the demands of power. Writers, he tells Brimmer,

> ". . . are not equipped for authority. . . . There is no substitute for will. Sometimes you have to fake will when you don't feel it at all."
> "I've had that experience."
> "You have to say, 'It's got to be like this—no other way'— even if you're not sure. A dozen times a week that happens to me. Situations where there is no real reason for anything. You pretend there is."
> "All leaders have felt that," said Brimmer. "Labor leaders, and certainly military leaders."[61]

Stahr stands as the center, the keystone of his world: in Fitzgerald's imagery, he is "the king,"[62] "the helmsman,"[63] "the oracle."[64] He himself constitutes the "unity."[65] When he delivers a judgment: "The oracle had spoken. There was nothing to question or argue. Stahr must be right always, not most of the time, but always—or the structure would melt down like gradual butter."[66] If the power of decision is, as many people would maintain, the essence of business success, then Stahr is one of the very few businessmen in fiction in whom we see the process of decision actually at work. His method, hinted at in the exchange with Brimmer, is magnificently expounded in his conversation with the pilot of the aircraft in the opening chapter:

> He was looking down at the mountains.
> "Suppose you were a railroad man," he said. "You have to send a train through there somewhere. Well, you get your surveyors' reports, and you find there's three or four or half a dozen gaps, and not one is better than the other. You've got to decide—on what basis? You can't test the best way—except by doing it. So you just do it."
> The pilot thought he had missed something.
> "How do you mean?"

[61] *Op. cit.,* p. 121.
[62] *Op. cit.,* p. 112.
[63] *Op. cit.,* p. 105.
[64] *Op. cit.,* p. 56.
[65] *Op. cit.,* p. 58.
[66] *Op. cit.,* p. 56.

"You choose some one way for no reason at all—because that mountain's pink or the blueprint is a better blue. You see?"

The pilot considered that this was very valuable advice. But he doubted if he'd ever be in a position to apply it.

"What I wanted to know," he told me ruefully, "is how he ever got to be Mr. Stahr."[67]

We know that Fitzgerald took this passage from an actual conversation, but that scarcely detracts from its impressiveness: indeed, we may see it as a mark of Fitzgerald's shrewdness, which we have already seen guiding him to a convincing presentation of worlds other than his own, that he should have recognized, despite the almost absurd simplicity of the remark, its revealing accuracy. Fitzgerald records that, listening to the speaker, he was impressed by "something more than shrewdness—by the largeness of what he thought."[68] It might be argued that the characterization of Stahr betrays traces of Fitzgerald's old tendency to uncritical hero-worship; certainly his attempt to invest Stahr with "largeness" in the last two paragraphs of Chapter One, whatever its rhetorical success, is not altogether substantiated by what we see of Stahr in action. The very solidity and concreteness of Fitzgerald's presentation of Stahr, the very convincingness of the scenes in what Cecilia calls "A Producer's Day," work against an acceptance of Stahr as a larger-than-life figure. However impressive his omni-competence, few of Stahr's individual decisions seem especially re-markable—apart, perhaps, from his insistence on making a picture that will lose money. The shadowiness with which Jay Gatsby is presented may raise occasional questions in the reader's mind, but it has undoubted artistic advantages.

If he had lived, Fitzgerald's completion and revision of *The Last Tycoon* might well have made this criticism irrelevant. There can be no question of the seriousness and thoroughness of Fitzgerald's attempt in his novel to present a detailed portrait of a specific industry and of a dominating figure in that industry. His portrayal of Stahr and of Stahr's world is scarcely less deliberate as social documentary than Dreiser's portrayal of Cowperwood. This is made clear by such notes as: "[Brady] is the monopolist at his worst—Stahr, in spite of the inevitable conservatism of the

---

[67] *Op. cit.,* pp. 19–20.
[68] Notes to *The Last Tycoon,* p. 135.

self-made man, is a paternalistic employer."[69] In his paternalism, indeed, Stahr seems rather reminiscent of Amherst in *The Fruit of the Tree,* but Fitzgerald has here an advantage over both Edith Wharton and Dreiser, and even over the author of his own earlier books, in his comprehensive knowledge of the world he presents and in his understanding, both as moralist and as novelist of manners, of all sides of his hero's personality.

Completed, *The Last Tycoon* would have been triumphant evidence of Fitzgerald's ability to write a social novel radically different from *The Great Gatsby* in both aim and method. Instead of relying on the brilliant poetic techniques which had enabled him to create the earlier novel's wholly convincing yet somewhat insubstantial world of manners, Fitzgerald in *The Last Tycoon* was attempting to reflect, through accretion of carefully selected detail, the whole fabric of the film industry as he knew it. *The Last Tycoon* would not necessarily have been a better book than *The Great Gatsby* nor more ambitious in scope than *Tender Is the Night,* but we may suspect that the Hollywood setting would have been not merely evoked, as the Long Island and New York settings are so skilfully evoked in *The Great Gatsby,* but recreated with complete solidity and understanding; while Monroe Stahr, for his part, would have become not only, with the possible exception of Dick Diver, the most fully drawn of Fitzgerald's characters, but one of the outstanding portraits of a businessman in the history of American fiction.

[69] *Op. cit.,* p. 140.

Midge Decter

Fitzgerald at the End

> "Yes," objected Amory, "but isn't it lack of will-
> power to let my imagination shinny on the wrong
> side?"—*This Side of Paradise.*

In 1938, so the story is often told, when Walter Wanger as-
signed the young Budd Schulberg to collaborate with F. Scott Fitzgerald on a script for a movie about Dartmouth, Schulberg said,
"Fitzgerald—I thought he was dead." So too, apparently, had the
group of drama students who produced "The Diamond as Big as
the Ritz" in a small room above the Pasadena Playhouse in 1939
and who were nonplussed and embarrassed to receive a back-
stage visit from Fitzgerald—in full evening dress—on opening
night. It was not so much that Fitzgerald had disappeared—he
was publishing a little in those days, though by his former standards very little; and after all *Tender Is the Night* had come out
only in 1934. It was that by some kind of unspoken consensus Fitzgerald was labeled "Finished" and put away. Perhaps at the time
there was a deep public courtesy involved in thinking him dead,
for his life, which neither he nor anyone else had ever succeeded
in separating from his work, had become an ugly spectacle,
marked by illness and Zelda's insanity and alcohol and failure.
The man—like the "Age" he had been saddled with representing,
like the American Dream itself—had finally collapsed. He was
violently and often viciously drunk much of the time. He was in
debt, apparently unable to work. And in 1936, when to do such a

Reprinted from Partisan Review, *XXVI (Spring 1959), 303–312, by permission of the author.*

thing was taken to be a clear sign of "selling out," he went off
to Hollywood to make some money and learn how to write successful movies. He himself had publicly announced his collapse
in three articles in *Esquire* ("The Crack-Up," "Handle With Care,"
"Pasting It Together"). The articles were of course in their very
nature a lie: true, they were the exploration of their author's feeling of personal ruin, his "spiritual bankruptcy," but they were
also among the strongest and most trenchant products of a writer
still capable of first-rate work.

When in 1940 Fitzgerald did die, he left behind six chapters
of a novel and voluminous notes for its completion. He left behind,
too, a feeling, and one that has persisted through the last eighteen
years of posthumous publication and reams of serious criticism
and acclaim, that some special redress of a wrong is due him. Or
if "redress" and "wrong" are too emphatic, that some kind of subtle
imbalance in the world's view of Fitzgerald must be set right. At
the end of his biography Arthur Mizener says,

> Like Gatsby . . . Fitzgerald loved reputation, the public acknowl-
> edgement of genuine achievement, with the impersonal magnanimity
> of a Renaissance prince. He lived, finally, to give that chaos in his
> head shape in his books and to see the knowledge that he had done
> so reflected back to him from the world. He died believing he had
> failed. Now we know better, and it is one of the final ironies of Fitz-
> gerald's career that he did not live to enjoy our knowledge.

That "now we know better," written ten years after Fitzgerald's
death and at the end of a painstaking biography, strikes the
curious personal note of apology—not so much for Fitzgerald
as *to* him—that sounds so often in the writing about him.

Now Sheilah Graham, who lived with Fitzgerald during his last
four years, has written her autobiography and the section about
their life together is also a moving personal defense of him.

Sheilah Graham was sent to Hollywood by the North American Newspaper Alliance to take over its syndicated movie gossip
column. Before coming to America from London, she had held
many posts in a rather stunning career of imposture and social
climbing: born Lily Sheil in London's East End and raised in an
orphanage, with no education, no experience and a bad accent, by
her late twenties she had managed to marry respectably, to make
something of a success on the musical comedy stage, to be presented at court, to crash the society of the English country aris-

tocracy, and finally to get in some semi-professional experience as a newspaper feature-writer. *Beloved Infidel* is unfortunately one of those autobiographical memoirs written in collaboration with Gerold Frank, in which all the author's real feelings, ideas, and responses to what has happened in life are buried beneath the most irritating narrative style ever invented. Everything in the book is reduced to an event coming at Miss Graham from the outside; her own part in it gets squeezed into a few handy mass-magazine formulas ("This was wonderful. This was the answer to everything" or "Even now, I wonder, who looked after me?")—so that the reader is left begging for a little relief from the specter of those wide-open baby-blue eyes. Nevertheless, merely from Sheilah Graham's story itself, and from the reconstruction all its flatly-told facts make inevitable, one can understand something of what must have been, what must be, the quality of this remarkable woman. There is, for instance, the fact that at each crucial moment of her life some man was waiting, and always just the man needed, to give her the protection and the training for the next audacious push of her ambition—the acme of which, I suppose, was reached in a proposal of marriage from the Marquess of Donegall, who has one of the oldest peerages in Britain. She was pretty; she was absolutely devoted to the climb; but these are somehow not enough to account for her astonishing career. Beyond them what she clearly had was grace, some Midas touch of the personality. However, what makes her most remarkable of all is that, with her gift of grace and given her lower-class romance about the rich and her totally expedient morality, she did not stop with the British aristocracy, the Marquess of Donegall, her fantasy of having children called the Earl of Belfast and the Lady Wendy of Chichester. She went on to an American newspaper career and to Fitzgerald. She never makes clear what prompted her to this last seemingly unaccountable step. She says she went to America looking for "love," but love is something no more easily to be found in New York than in London, and her street sense must have told her so even if her romantic literary ego no longer does. She describes a very unpretty scene between Randolph Churchill and Charlie Chaplin at a posh London restaurant in which Churchill was overbearing and arrogant and Chaplin was obsequious, and talks of her own shock at discovering that even genius must bow to the blood. Years earlier, as a hungry young girl strolling down Piccadilly night after night, money and titles had seemed the best the world could offer. But when she got access to them, she wanted something better, something by whose terms Charlie Chaplin did not have to be patronized nor she to be a liar. And when she met Fitzgerald in Hollywood, she was able to decide almost immediately that he was what she wanted. She had never known anyone like Fitzgerald—writers and literary intellectuals during her brief stay in New York had intimidated her—but her infallible instinct must have seized on what even by the time she sat down to do this book she could only express indirectly and cumulatively: that with Fitzgerald she had come to the *very* best.

Fitzgerald educated her. He would prepare detailed reading lists for her, discuss her assignments when she had read them; they listened to music, read criticism, and they called it the "F. Scott Fitzgerald College of One." If there is something embarrassing and pathetic in the way she talks about her studies ("I thought, suddenly, I will not be in this position again. They discuss Franz Kafka and T. S. Eliot and Wallenstein and Richelieu and the Thirty Years' War and I sit on the outside, looking in.") and about the reading lists themselves, there is also something new and striking in such a picture of Fitzgerald: the man who with Edmund Wilson and other friends seemed humbly to accept his role as intellectual inferior, whose spelling was a public joke, had with delight and great energy taken on the role of "intellectual conscience" to someone else. And so much of what Miss Graham presents of Fitzgerald comes at us this way. She found him all by herself. She hadn't known who he was; she hadn't read his books. For her there were no staled or hackneyed public images, no old history, coming between them. This is why she can make us *see* the things his friends and Mr. Mizener could only refer to in writing about him: his wit, his charm, his astonishing profligacy of spirit, and his self-hatred. Even his drunks, which had until this book become distant and legendary—one of them already the subject of a famous novel and play—are made real; meaner, nastier, more shocking, perhaps, than it had become necessary to think—but for the first time the real behavior of a real man. The F. Scott Fitzgerald Miss Graham found because she looked for herself and because she had the proper need of him was a strong man. He educated her; he gave her values.

The final twist about the Fitzgerald we see through Sheilah Graham's eyes is that for her he had become the exponent of the values he embodied as a creative artist—he who had seemed so helpless to come to terms with them himself.

Perhaps nobody's values have been subjected to the kind of

critical scrutiny Fitzgerald's have. Virtually everything he wrote raises in the minds of his readers the question of his own relation to the moral and spiritual emptiness of the ethos he so poignantly chronicles. Does he stand inside or outside the terms by which his characters judge the world and on account of which they are doomed? It would take only a small failure of imagination, only a minute but essential shutting off of sympathy, to find Fitzgerald's life doomed as are the lives of his characters, and for something like the same reason: not because he seemed so much to dignify their illusions but because the illusions he dignified were so cheap.

Like Sheilah Graham, Fitzgerald had done a great deal of traveling to get to the Hollywood where they met. If her journey can be described as one straight up, then his was one down through the bottom and out the other side. Both of them had displayed great courage, but hers, of the nervy kind, risked only not succeeding; he had risked failure. In order to be something it was impossible for him to be—what he called "an entire man in the Goethe-Byron-Shaw tradition, with an opulent American touch"—he had handicapped himself and his thick, easy, generous talent at every turn, and in the end probably only left one book and a few stories that will outlast the radical social changes of the next few decades. The "entire man" he dreamed of was a man always to be remembered as much for what he was as for what he did, in whom it would be impossible to distinguish the boundary between personality and achievement, a "figure." But Fitzgerald was born into a world in which everyone *begins* as a figure. In St. Paul the confusion between personality and achievement, though on another level, comes easy. You do not attain it, you fall victim to it. In a place like the snowy, red-cheeked, robust, self-made world of "The Ice Palace" and "Winter Dreams," what you do is the public definition of what you are; the exclusive and exhaustive one. And the problem, if you do something so indefinable and subversive of order as write, is not to impose a public image but precisely to protect your private personality from the exactions of an image foisted on you, as it were, almost at birth. Under the circumstances, Fitzgerald did not have to become the embodiment of the Jazz Age, or anything else—without some great effort he could not have avoided it. In seeking the old unity of life and art, what he achieved was an immensely fertile but almost fatally costly confusion of experience with the meaning of experience, of identification with empathy. He became someone for whom there was neither escape from innocence nor retreat from consciousness.

That he kept the cost from being fatal, that he made his self-conscious innocence work for him, is after all only an ambiguous victory. Nevertheless, it is a victory, and one to which we owe a unique, irreplaceable record of what Americans come from and what they must all get through in order to grow up. In some ways the purest product of Fitzgerald's special gift for tossing experience at you still raw and just unwrapped from the nerves is *This Side of Paradise*. Certainly the book is a chaos, an adolescent riot of literary mismatched limbs, changing voice and sexual incompetence. However, it is wild and profuse not only because Fitzgerald was then a totally undisciplined writer but also because the novel itself so perfectly achieves an identification with the disorganizing and unmanageable predicament of Amory Blaine. Amory's predicament often seems like child's-play, but Fitzgerald's keen inside sense of it, his respect for its urgency, cuts through the triviality of its specific content and makes us see it for what it really is: an expression of the great American conflict between a meanness of culture and a grandeur of pretension—the struggle between the coarseness of attitude that gives Americans so much will to deal with the world and the faint, delicate image of beauty that is to be the object of that will.

This Side of Paradise lacks even the pretense of a plot, and the fact that is it not plotted derives from a conscious refusal on Fitzgerald's part to have it so. He does not know what must become of Amory and therefore cannot make what happens to him fit into some pattern of becoming. "I know myself—but that is all!" is Amory's last cry—and it is Fitzgerald's cry too. Nor does he really plot the later novels (of course, and always, excepting *Gatsby*). Anthony Patch and Dick Diver get older; their lives themselves have taken on more form, and therefore the books do. Fitzgerald is able to take these characters farther—he takes them, in fact, up to the point of dissolution. But he does not really either get beyond them in time and look back nor outside them and look in. He is never recreating life but only making a progress report on it.

With *Gatsby* something different happened. Gatsby is not a character in Fitzgerald's sense, not a life in the process of unfolding. Gatsby is an idea. In writing the book Fitzgerald was clearly seized by a vision, a pure distillation of his relation to something large and abstract—to America—and at the end of this vision there was Gatsby's corpse floating in the pool. The corpse, the abstraction, gave him the freedom he never sought or took elsewhere to direct all the movement that led to it.

Tender Is the Night, then, is Fitzgerald's last progress report on his odyssey into figuredom. The report is a bad one. Dick Diver is finished, and finished in a way seemingly prophetic for Fitzgerald: he is no longer useful to those it had become the meaning of his life to serve. The year *Tender Is the Night* came out, Fitzgerald and Zelda published a little piece ("Auction—Model 1934") taking inventory of the acquisitions of their life together. They unpack their household goods and find themselves left with a heap of attic-bound junk, the bric-a-brac of former good times and enthusiasms and wastefulness. The article is written in a tone rather lyric and tender, but the inventory has the finality of a last counting. They end by saying: "We shall keep it all—the tangible remnant of the four hundred thousand we made from hard words and spent with easy ones these fifteen years. And the collection, after all, is just about as valuable now as the Polish and Peruvian bonds of our thriftier friends."

There is no human stance so attractive as the refusal to be thrifty. To the Midwestern boy Fitzgerald was for such a long time, using up with easy words what had been earned with hard ones became a point of self-respect. More than that, it must have seemed the only possiblity for purging himself of the littleness, the spirit of husbandry, bred so inescapably in the struggle of his forebears to make some permanent mark on the wide, shifting middle reaches of a vast continent. Surely in his projected ideal triumvirate of the "entire man," it was the force of Byron that Fitzgerald felt most keenly. And like Byron he was to write one book out of the wisdom that comes with knowing the self has given all it had to give and that therefore it need give nothing: *The Last Tycoon* is his *Don Juan.*

If the collection of stuff that in only a few years came to be relics of an ancient and dead past was no more worthless than the Polish and Peruvian bonds of the prudent, unlike the bonds it had to be paid for twice. It was yet to present Fitzgerald with a bill in the form of a terrible crisis of spirit. Fitzgerald was to be forty years old and totally unable to write—he who had sometimes knocked out stories in a matter of hours— before his romantic conscience could decide he had paid enough and was now permitted to muster the thrift to save himself. *The Last Tycoon* and the Pat Hobby stories, written during the time with Sheilah Graham, signal his capitulation—or if you will his advance—to a new role. He was now to be that most intensely partial, un-"entire" of men, an artist.

He was ashamed of the new demands he felt obliged to make and spoke of them with heavy irony: "And if you were dying of starvation outside my window, I would go out quickly and give you the smile and the voice (if no longer the hand) and stick around till somebody raised a nickel to phone for the ambulance, that is if I thought there would be any copy in it for me. I have now at last become a writer only." To Sheilah Graham he spoke of his demands not at all. But though the best of the times they had together were often idyllic, often gay, though Fitzgerald was tender and infinitely sympathetic, what she says makes it clear that *happiness* for him then was work.

The Last Tycoon finished might have turned out to be his best novel or his worst, but it would have been a novel different in kind from all the others. The completed chapters and notes are written by a Fitzgerald who had finally settled for the wisdom that can come this side of paradise and for the comforts of the traditional relations between a novelist and his society: the one not taking meaning from, but giving meaning to, the other.

Selected Bibliography

FITZGERALD'S WORKS (* indicates book is available in paperback edition)

This Side of Paradise, * Scribner's, New York, 1920.

Flappers and Philosophers, Scribner's, New York, 1920. ("The Offshore Pirate," "The Ice Palace," "Head and Shoulders," "The Cut-Glass Bowl," "Bernice Bobs Her Hair," "Benediction," "Dalyrimple Goes Wrong," "The Four Fists.")

The Beautiful and Damned, * Scribner's, New York, 1922.

Tales of the Jazz Age, * Scribner's, New York, 1922. ("The Jelly-Bean," "The Camel's Back," "May Day," "Porcelain and Pink," "The Diamond as Big as the Ritz," "The Curious Case of Benjamin Button," "Tarquin of Cheapside," "O Russet Witch!" "The Lees of Happiness," "Mr. Icky," "Jemina.")

The Vegetable, Scribner's, New York, 1923.

The Great Gatsby, * Scribner's, New York, 1925; Chatto & Windus, London, 1926. Reprinted with a new introduction by Fitzgerald—Modern Library, New York, 1934.

All the Sad Young Men, Scribner's, New York, 1926. ("The Rich Boy," "Winter Dreams," "The Baby Party," "Absolution," "Rags Martin—Jones and the Pr-nce of W-les," "The Adjuster," "Hot and Cold Blood," "'The Sensible Thing,'" "Gretchen's Forty Winks.")

Tender Is the Night, * Scribner's, New York, 1934; Chatto & Windus, London, 1934. Republished "With the Author's Final Revisions," ed. Malcolm Cowley—Scribner's, New York, 1951.

Taps at Reveille, * Scribner's, New York, 1935. (*Basil:* "The Scandal Detectives," "The Freshest Boy," "He Thinks He's Wonderful," "The Captured Shadow," "The Perfect Life"; *Josephine:* "First Blood," "A Nice Quiet Place," "A Woman with a Past"; "Crazy Sunday," "Two Wrongs," "The Night of Chancellorsville," "The Last of the Belles," "Majesty," "Family in the Wind," "A Short Trip Home," "One Interne," "The Fiend," "Babylon Revisited.")

The Last Tycoon, * ed. Edmund Wilson, Scribner's, New York, 1941.

The Crack-Up,* ed. Edmund Wilson, New Directions, Norfolk, Conn., 1945.

The Stories of F. Scott Fitzgerald,* introduction by Malcolm Cowley, Scribner's, New York, 1951.

Afternoon of an Author,* ed. Arthur Mizener, Scribner's, New York, 1958; Bodley Head, London, 1958.

Babylon Revisited and Other Stories,* Scribner's, New York, 1960. ("The Ice Palace," "May Day," "The Diamond as Big as the Ritz," "Winter Dreams," "Absolution," "The Rich Boy," "The Freshest Boy," "Babylon Revisited," "Crazy Sunday," "The Long Way Out.")

The Mystery of the Raymond Mortgage, Random House, New York, 1960.

The Pat Hobby Stories, introduction by Arnold Gingrich, Scribner's, New York, 1962.

The Apprentice Fiction of F. Scott Fitzgerald, 1909–1917, ed. John Kuehl, Rutgers University Press, New Brunswick, N.J., 1965.

Thoughtbook of Francis Scott Key Fitzgerald, introduction by John Kuehl, Princeton University Library, Princeton, 1965.

The Portable F. Scott Fitzgerald, selected by Dorothy Parker and introduction by John O'Hara, Viking, New York, 1949.

The Bodley Head Scott Fitzgerald, 6 Vols, Bodley Head, London, 1958–1963.

The Fitzgerald Reader,* ed. with an introduction by Arthur Mizener, Scribner's, New York, 1963.

LETTERS AND BIOGRAPHICAL SOURCES

As Ever, Scott Fitzgerald, ed. Matthew J. Bruccoli, Lippincott, Philadelphia, 1972. Correspondence with his agent, Harold Ober.

Dear Scott/Dear Max; the Fitzgerald-Perkins Correspondence, ed. John Kuehl and Jackson Bryer, Scribner's, New York, 1971.

Graham, Sheilah: *College of One,* Viking, New York, 1967.

————: *The Rest of the Story,* Coward-McCann, New York, 1964.

Graham, Sheilah, and Gerold Frank: *Beloved Infidel,* Holt, Rinehart & Winston, New York, 1958.

Letters to his Daughter, introduction by Frances Fitzgerald Lanahan, Scribner's, New York, 1965. From Turnbull's edition of *The Letters.*

The Letters of F. Scott Fitzgerald, ed. Andrew Turnbull, Scribner's, New York, 1963; Bodley Head, London, 1964.

Mayfield, Sara: *Exiles from Paradise: Zelda and Scott Fitzgerald,* Delacorte Press, New York, 1971.

Milford, Nancy: *Zelda,* Harper & Row, New York, 1970.

Mizener, Arthur: *The Far Side of Paradise,* Houghton Mifflin, Boston, 1951, rev. ed., 1965.

Piper, Henry Dan: *F. Scott Fitzgerald/A Critical Portrait,* Holt, Rinehart & Winston, New York, 1965.

Turnbull, Andrew: *Scott Fitzgerald,* Scribner's, New York, 1962.

SPECIAL JOURNALS

Bruccoli, Matthew J. (ed.): *Fitzgerald Newsletter,* 1958–68. Reprinted—Microcard Editions, Washington D.C., 1969.

Bruccoli, Matthew J. and C. E. Frazer Clark, Jr. (eds.):*Fitzgerald/ Hemingway Annual,* Microcard Editions, Washington, D.C., 1969–. Individual articles appearing in the above sources are not included in this bibliography.

BIBLIOGRAPHIES AND CHECKLISTS

Beebe, Maurice and Jackson R. Bryer, "Criticism of F. Scott Fitzgerald: A Selected Checklist," *Modern Fiction Studies,* 82–94, Spring 1961.

Bruccoli, Matthew J.: *Checklist of F. Scott Fitzgerald,* Charles E. Merrill, Columbus, Ohio, 1970.

————: *F. Scott Fitzgerald: A Descriptive Bibliography,* University of Pittsburgh Press, Pittsburgh, 1972.

Bryer, Jackson R.: *The Critical Reputation of F. Scott Fitzgerald,* Archon, New Haven, Conn., 1967.

————: "F. Scott Fitzgerald," in *Fifteen Modern American Authors: A Survey of Research and Criticism,* Duke University Press, Durham, N.C., 1969.

Fitzgerald Newsletter, Nos. 1–40 (1958–1968). Quarterly checklist in each number. Thereafter in *Fitzgerald/Hemingway Annual,* 1969–.

BOOKS

Bruccoli, Matthew J: *The Composition of Tender Is the Night,* University of Pittsburgh Press, Pittsburgh, 1963.

Bruccoli, Matthew J., and Jackson R. Bryer: *Fitzgerald in His Own*

Time: A Miscellany, Kent State University Press, Kent, Ohio, 1971.

Cowley, Malcolm, and Robert Cowley: *Fitzgerald and the Jazz Age,* Scribner's, New York, 1966.

Cross, K. G. W.: *Scott Fitzgerald,* Oliver & Boyd, Edinburgh and London, 1964; Barnes & Noble, New York, 1966.

Eble, Kenneth: *F. Scott Fitzgerald,* Twayne, New York, 1963.

Fitzgerald, Zelda: *Save Me the Waltz,* Scribner's, New York, 1932; Southern Illinois University Press, Carbondale, Ill., 1967.

Goldhurst, William: *F. Scott Fitzgerald and his Contemporaries.* World, Cleveland and New York, 1963.

Hoffman, Frederick J. (ed.): *The Great Gatsby: a Study,* Scribner's, New York, 1962.

Kazin, Alfred: *F. Scott Fitzgerald: The Man and His Work,* World, Cleveland and New York, 1951.

LaHood, Marvin J. (ed.): *Tender is the Night: Essays in Criticism,* Indiana University Press, Bloomington, Ind., 1969.

Latham, Aaron: *Crazy Sundays: F. Scott Fitzgerald in Hollywood,* Viking, New York, 1970.

Lehan, Richard D: *F. Scott Fitzgerald and the Craft of Fiction,* Southern Illinois University Press, Carbondale, Ill., 1966.

Lockridge, Ernest, (ed.): *Twentieth Century Interpretations of The Great Gatsby,* Prentice-Hall, Englewood Cliffs, N.J., 1968.

Miller, James E., Jr.: *The Fictional Technique of F. Scott Fitzgerald,* Nijhoff, The Hague, 1957; Englarged edition—*F. Scott Fitzgerald: His Art and His Technique,* New York University Press, New York, 1964.

Mizener, Arthur, (ed.): *F. Scott Fitzgerald: A Collection of Critical Essays,* Prentice-Hall, Englewood Cliffs, N.J., 1963.

Perosa, Sergio: *The Art of F. Scott Fitzgerald,* University of Michigan Press, Ann Arbor, Mich., 1965.

Shain, Charles E: *F. Scott Fitzgerald,* University of Minnesota Press, Minneapolis, 1961.

Sklar, Robert: *F. Scott Fitzgerald: The Last Laocoön,* Oxford University Press, New York, 1967.

Stern, Milton R.: *The Golden Moment: The Novels of F. Scott Fitzgerald,* University of Illinois Press, Urbana, Ill., 1969.

ARTICLES

Aldridge, John W.: "Fitzgerald—The Horror and the Vision of

Paradise," in *After the Lost Generation,* McGraw-Hill, New York, 1951, pp. 44–58.

Astro, Richard: *"Vandover and the Brute* and *The Beautiful and Damned:* A Search for Thematic and Stylistic Reinterpretations," *Modern Fiction Studies,* **14,** 397–413, Winter 1968–69.

Babb, Howard S.: *"The Great Gatsby* and the Grotesque," *Criticism,* **5,** 336–48, Fall 1963.

Baldwin, Charles C.: "F. Scott Fitzgerald," in *The Men Who Make Our Novels* (rev. ed.), Dodd, Mead, New York, 1924, pp. 166–73.

Barrett, William: "Fitzgerald and America," *Partisan Review,* **18,** 345–53, May-June 1951.

Berryman, John: "F. Scott Fitzgerald," *Kenyon Review,* **8,** 103–12, Winter 1946.

Bewley, Marius: "Scott Fitzgerald's Criticism of America," *Sewanee Review,* **62,** 223–46, Spring 1954.

Bicknell, John W.: "The Waste Land of F. Scott Fitzgerald," *Virginia Quarterly Review,* **30,** 556–72, Autumn 1954.

Bishop, John Peale: "The Missing All," *Virginia Quarterly Review,* **13,** 106–21, Winter 1937.

Blackshear, Helen F.: "Mama Sayre, Scott Fitzgerald's Mother-in-law," *Georgia Review,* **19,** 465–470, Winter 1965.

Boyd, Ernest: "F. Scott Fitzgerald," in *Portraits: Real and Imaginary,* Cape, London, 1924, pp. 217–26.

Boyd, Thomas Alexander: "Literary Libels—Francis Scott Key Fitzgerald," *St. Paul Daily News,* March 5, 1922; March 12, 1922; March 19, 1922.

Bruccoli, Matthew J.: "Bibliographical Notes on F. Scott Fitzgerald's *The Beautiful and Damned,*" *Studies in Bibliography,* **13,** 258–61, 1960.

———: "Material for a Centenary Edition of *Tender Is the Night,*" *Studies in Bibliography,* **17,** 177–93, 1964.

———: *"Tender Is the Night* and the Reviewers," *Modern Fiction Studies,* **7,** 49–54, Spring 1961.

Bryer, Jackson R.: "F. Scott Fitzgerald and the State of American Letters in 1921," *Modern Fiction Studies,* **12,** 265–67, Summer 1966.

———. "A Psychiatrist Reviews *Tender Is the Night,*" *Literature and Psychology,* **16,** 198–99, 1966.

Burnam, Tom: "The Eyes of Dr. Eckleburg: A Reexamination of *The Great Gatsby,*" *College English,* **14,** 7–12, October 1952.

Cardwell, Guy A.: "The Lyric World of Scott Fitzgerald," *Virginia Quarterly Review,* **38,** 229–323, Spring 1962.

Carlisle, E. Fred: "The Triple Vision of Nick Carraway," *Modern Fiction Studies,* **11,** 351–360, Winter 1965–66.

Coleman, Thomas C.: "Nicole Warren Diver and Scott Fitzgerald: The Girl and the Egotist," *Studies in the Novel,* **3,** 34–43, Spring 1971.

Cowley, Malcolm: "Of Clocks and Calendars," *New Republic,* Mar. 17, 1941, pp. 376–77.

———: "Third Act and Epilogue," *New Yorker,* June 30, 1945, pp. 53–58.

———: "The Scott Fitzgerald Story," *New Republic,* Feb. 12, 1951, pp. 17–20.

———: "Fitzgerald: The Double Man," *Saturday Review,* Feb. 24, 1951, pp. 9–10, 42–45.

———: "F. Scott Fitzgerald: The Romance of Money," *Western Review,* **17,** 245–55, Summer 1953.

Decter, Midge: "Fitzgerald at the End," *Partisan Review,* **26,** 303–12, Spring 1959.

Dos Passos, John: "Fitzgerald and the Press," *New Republic,* Feb. 17, 1941, p. 213.

Doyno, Victor: "Patterns in *The Great Gatsby,*" *Modern Fiction Studies,* **12,** 415–26, Winter 1966.

Dyson, A. E.: "*The Great Gatsby:* Thirty-Six Years After," *Modern Fiction Studies,* **7,** 37–48, Spring 1961.

Eble, Kenneth E.: "Scott Fitzgerald, Seriously," *Columbia University Forum,* **5,** 38–41, Summer 1962.

———: "The Craft of Revision: *The Great Gatsby,*" *American Literature,* **36,** 315–26, November 1964.

Ellis, James: "Fitzgerald's Fragmented Hero: Dick Diver," *University Review,* **32,** 43–49, October 1965.

Fiedler, Leslie A.: "Notes on F. Scott Fitzgerald," *New Leader,* Apr. 9, 1951, pp. 20–21; Apr. 16, 1951, pp. 23–24.

Forrey, Robert: "Negroes in the Fiction of F. Scott Fitzgerald," *Phylon,* **28,** 293–98, 1967.

Fraser, John: "Dust and Dreams in *The Great Gatsby,*" *Journal of English Literary History,* **32,** 554–564, 1965.

Friedrich, Otto: "Reappraisals—F. Scott Fitzgerald: Money, Money, Money," *American Scholar,* **29,** 382–405, Summer 1960.

Frohock, W. M.: "Morals, Manners, and Scott Fitzgerald," *Southwest Review,* **40,** 220–28, Summer 1955.

Fussell, Edwin S.: "Fitzgerald's Brave New World," *English Literary History,* **19,** 291–306, December 1952.

G[ingrich], A[rnold]: "Publisher's Page—Will the Real Scott

Fitzgerald Please Stand Up and Be Counted?" *Esquire,* Dec. 1964, pp. 8, 10, 12, 16.

————: "Scott, Ernest and Whoever," *Esquire,* Dec. 1966, pp. 186–89, 322–25.

Gindin, James: "Gods and Fathers in F. Scott Fitzgerald's Novels," *Modern Language Quarterly,* **30,** 64–85, March 1969.

Goodwin, Donald W.: "The Alcoholism of F. Scott Fitzgerald," *Journal of the American Medical Association,* **212,** 86–90, Apr. 6, 1970.

Gross, Barry: "The Dark Side of Twenty-five: Fitzgerald and *The Beautiful and Damned," Bucknell Review,* **16,** 40–52, December 1968.

Gross, Seymour L.: "Fitzgerald's 'Babylon Revisited,'" *College English,* **25,** 128–35, November 1963.

Hanzo, Thomas A.: "The Theme and the Narrator of *The Great Gatsby," Modern Fiction Studies,* **2,** 183–90, Winter 1956–57.

Harding, D. W.: "Scott Fitzgerald," *Scrutiny,* **18,** 166–74, Winter 1951–52.

Harvey, W. J.: "Theme and Texture in *The Great Gatsby," English Studies,* **38,** 12–20, February 1957.

Hearne, Laura Guthrie: "A Summer With F. Scott Fitzgerald," *Esquire,* Dec. 1964, pp. 160–65, 232, 236–237, 240, 242, 246, 250, 252, 254–58, 260.

Kahn, Sy: "*This Side of Paradise:* The Pageantry of Disillusion," *Midwest Quarterly,* **7,** 177–94, Winter 1966.

Kallich, Martin: "F. Scott Fitzgerald: Money or Morals," *University of Kansas City Review,* **15,** 271–80, Summer 1949.

Kazin, Alfred: "Fitzgerald: An American Confession," *Quarterly Review of Literature,* **2,** 341–46, 1945.

Kreuter, Kent, and Gretchen Kreuter: "The Moralism of the Later Fitzgerald," *Modern Fiction Studies,* **7,** 71–81, Spring 1961.

Kuehl, John R.: "Scott Fitzgerald: Romantic and Realist," *Texas Studies in Literature and Language,* **1,** 412–26, Autumn 1959.

————: "Scott Fitzgerald's Reading," *Princeton University Library Chronicle,* **22,** 58–89, Winter 1961.

————: "Scott Fitzgerald's Critical Opinions," *Modern Fiction Studies,* **7,** 3–18, Spring 1961.

Lanahan, Frances Scott Fitzgerald: "Princeton and my Father," *Princeton Alumni Weekly,* March 9, 1956, pp. 8–9.

Lauter, Paul: "Plato's Stepchildren, Gatsby and Cohn," *Modern Fiction Studies,* **9,** 338–46, Winter 1963–64.

Liebling, A. J.: "Books: Amory, We're Beautiful," *New Yorker,* May 19, 1951, pp. 129–36.

Lisca, Peter: "Nick Carraway and the Imagery of Disorder," *Twentieth Century Literature,* **13,** 18–28, April 1967.

Long, Robert E.: "The Great Gatsby and the Tradition of Joseph Conrad," *Texas Studies in Literature and Language,* **8,** 257–76, 407–22, Summer and Fall 1966.

MacKendrick, Paul L.: *"The Great Gatsby* and Trimalchio," *Classical Journal,* **45,** 307–14, April 1950.

Male, Roy R.: "'Babylon Revisited': A Story of the Exile's Return," *Studies in Short Fiction,* **2,** 270–77, Spring 1965.

McCall, Dan E.: "'The Self-Same Song That Found a Path': Keats and *The Great Gatsby,"* *American Literature* **42,** 421–30, January 1971.

Milford, Nancy: "The Golden Dream of Zelda Fitzgerald," *Harper's,* January 1969, pp. 46–53.

Millgate, Michael: "Scott Fitzgerald as Social Novelist: Statement and Technique in *The Last Tycoon,"* *English Studies,* **43,** 29–34, February 1962.

Mizener, Arthur: "The F. Scott Fitzgerald Papers," *Princeton University Library Chronicle,* **12,** 190–95, Summer 1951.

———: "The Maturity of Scott Fitzgerald," *Sewanee Review,* **67,** 658–75, Autumn 1959.

———: "Scott Fitzgerald and Edith Wharton," *London Times Literary Supplement,* July 7, 1966, p. 595; reply by Andrew Turnbull, Sept. 29, 1966, p. 899.

———: "Scott Fitzgerald and the 1920s," *Minnesota Review,* **1,** 161–74, Winter 1961.

———: "Scott Fitzgerald and the Top Girl," *Atlantic,* Mar. 1961, pp. 55–60.

Mok, Michel: "The Other Side of Paradise," *New York Post,* Sept. 25, 1936, pp. 1, 15.

Morris, Wright: "The Ability to Function: A Reappraisal of Fitzgerald and Hemingway," *New World Writing,* **13,** 34–43, June 1958.

Nardin, James T.: "Points of Moral Reference: A Comparative Study of Edith Wharton and F. Scott Fitzgerald," in *English Institute Essays: 1949,* ed. Alan S. Downer, Columbia University Press, New York, 1950, pp. 147–76.

Nason, Thelma: "Afternoon (and Evening) of an Author," *Johns Hopkins Magazine,* **21,** 2–15, February 1970.

O'Hara, John: "Scott Fitzgerald—Odds and Ends," *New York Times Book Review,* July 8, 1945, p. 3.

Ornstein, Robert: "Scott Fitzgerald's Fable of East and West," *College English,* **18,** 139–43, December 1956.

Piper, Henry Dan: "Fitzgerald's Cult of Disillusion," *American Quarterly*, **3**, 69–80, Spring 1951.

Powers, J. F.: "Dealer in Diamonds and Rhinestones," *Commonweal*, Aug. 10, 1945, pp. 408–410.

Richards, Robert, and Chris Richards: "Feeling in *The Great Gatsby*," *Western Humanities Review*, **21**, 257–65, Summer 1967.

Riddel, Joseph N.: "F. Scott Fitzgerald, the Jamesian Inheritance, and the Morality of Fiction," *Modern Fiction Studies*, **11**, 331–50, Winter 1965–66.

Ring, Frances Kroll: "My Boss, Scott Fitzgerald," *Los Angeles Magazine*, **7**, 34–36, January 1964.

Robbins, J. Albert: "Fitzgerald and the Simple Inarticulate Farmer," *Modern Fiction Studies*, **7**, 365–69, Winter 1961–62.

Rosenfeld, Paul: "F. Scott Fitzgerald," in *Men Seen,* Dial Press, New York 1925, pp. 215–24.

Ross, Alan: "Rumble Among the Drums—F. Scott Fitzgerald (1896–1940) and the Jazz Age," *Horizon*, **18**, 420–35, December 1948.

Samuels, Charles Thomas: "The Greatness of 'Gatsby,'" *Massachusetts Review*, **7**, 783–94, Autumn 1966.

Savage, D. S.: "The Significance of F. Scott Fitzgerald," *Arizona Quarterly*, **8**, 197–210, Autumn 1952.

Schneider, Daniel J.: "Color-Symbolism in *The Great Gatsby*," *University Review*, **31**, 13–17, October 1964.

Schoenwald, Richard L.: "F. Scott Fitzgerald as John Keats," *M.I.T. Publications in the Humanities*, **28**, 12–21, 1958.

Schorer, Mark: "Some Relationships: Gertrude Stein, Sherwood Anderson, F. Scott Fitzgerald, and Ernest Hemingway," in *The World We Imagine,* Farrar, Straus & Giroux, New York, 1968, pp. 299–382.

Schulberg, Budd: "In Hollywood," *New Republic*, Mar. 3, 1941, pp. 311–12.

———: "Old Scott: The Mask, the Myth, and the Man," *Esquire*, Jan. 1961, pp. 97–101.

Scrimgeour, Gary J.: "Against 'The Great Gatsby,'" *Criticism*, **8**, 75–86, Winter 1966.

Spencer, Benjamin T.: "Fitzgerald and the American Ambivalence," *South Atlantic Quarterly*, **66**, 367–81, Summer 1967.

Stallman, R. W.: "Gatsby and the Hole in Time," "Conrad and *The Great Gatsby*," "By the Dawn's Early Light *Tender Is the Night*," in *The Houses That James Built and Other Literary Studies,* Michigan State University Press, East Lansing, Mich., 1961, pp. 131–72.

Tanselle, G. Thomas, and Jackson R. Bryer: *"The Great Gatsby*— a Study in Literary Reputation," *New Mexico Quarterly,* **33,** 409–25, Winter 1963–64.

Taylor, Douglas: *"The Great Gatsby:* Style and Myth," *University of Kansas City Review,* **20,** 30–40, Autumn 1953.

Taylor, Dwight: "Scott Fitzgerald in Hollywood," *Harper's,* Mar. 1959, pp. 67–71.

Thurber, James: "'Scott in Thorns,'" *The Reporter,* Apr. 17, 1951, pp. 35–38.

Tomkins, Calvin. "Living Well Is the Best Revenge," *New Yorker,* July 28, 1962, pp. 31–32, 34, 36, 38, 43–44, 46–47, 49–50, 52, 54, 56–59.

Trilling, Lionel: "F. Scott Fitzgerald," *The Nation,* Aug. 25, 1945, pp. 182–184.

Troy, William: "Scott Fitzgerald—The Authority of Failure," *Accent,* **6,** 56–60, Autumn 1945.

Vanderbilt, Kermit: "James, Fitzgerald, and the American Self-Image," *Massachusetts Review,* **6,** 289–304, Winter–Spring 1965.

Wanning, Andrews: "Fitzgerald and His Brethren," *Partisan Review,* **12,** 545–51, Fall 1945.

Warren, Dale: "(Signed) F. S. F.," *Princeton University Library Chronicle,* **25,** 129–36, Winter 1964.

Watkins, Floyd C.: "Fitzgerald's Jay Gatz and Young Ben Franklin," *New England Quarterly,* **27,** 249–52, June 1954.

Weir, Charles, Jr.: "'An Invite With Gilded Edges,'" *Virginia Quarterly Review,* **20,** 100–113, Winter 1944.

Wescott, Glenway: "The Moral of Scott Fitzgerald," *New Republic,* Feb. 17, 1941, pp. 213–17.

Westbrook, J. S.: "Nature and Optics in *The Great Gatsby,"* *American Literature,* **32,** 78–84, Mar. 1960.

White, Eugene: "The 'Intricate Destiny' of Dick Diver," *Modern Fiction Studies,* **7,** 55–62, Spring 1961.

Whitehead, Lee M.: *"Tender Is the Night* and George Herbert Mead," *Literature and Psychology,* **15,** 180–191, Summer 1965.

Wilson, Edmund: "A Weekend at Ellerslie," in *The Shores of Light,* Farrar, Straus, New York, 1952, pp. 373–83.

———: "Imaginary Conversations, II: Mr. Van Wyck Brooks and Mr. Scott Fitzgerald," *New Republic,* Apr. 30, 1924, pp. 249–54.

———: "The Literary Spotlight—VI: F. Scott Fitzgerald," *The Bookman* (New York), **55,** 20–25, March 1922.

Yates, Donald A.: "The Road to 'Paradise': Fitzgerald's Literary Apprenticeship," *Modern Fiction Studies,* **7,** 19–31, Spring 1961.